THE FIRST
EGYPTIANS

McKissick Museum
and the
Earth Sciences and Resources Institute

The University of South Carolina

The Narmer Palette, a carved triangular-shaped slab of dark green slate, commemorates the unification of the "Two Lands" of Egypt. On one side, King Narmer wears the high-peaked crown of Upper Egypt while ritually bashing the head of a northern enemy beneath the protective gaze of the hawk god, Horus. The reverse face depicts Narmer bedecked in the red crown of Lower Egypt, impassively reviewing his beheaded opponents on the battlefield. He is accompanied by his allies and members of the court while a rampant bull, a traditional symbol of the Pharaoh, smashes the walls of an enemy town. Below the red-crowned Narmer are two intertwined mythical animals, thought to represent the unification of Upper and Lower Egypt. The elements seen on the Narmer Palette are arranged in rows called registers just as are seen in later tomb paintings, reliefs and hierogylphic writing.

The Narmer Palette was found at Hierakonpolis by J. E. Quibell in 1897-98.

T H E F I R S T
EGYPTIANS

An exhibition
organized by McKissick Museum
and the
Earth Sciences and Resources
Institute
of the University of South Carolina

Project Director
Michael Allen Hoffman

Editors
Karin L. Willoughby
and
Elizabeth B. Stanton

Catalogue funded in part
by the National Endowment for the Humanities.

©1988, by The McKissick Museum,
The University of South Carolina

Library of Congress Publication Data is available.
87-063464
ISBN 0-938983-04-0

LENDERS

We are grateful to the following lenders for their gracious contribution to this travelling exhibition:

The Brooklyn Museum
Brooklyn, New York

The Charleston Museum
Charleston, South Carolina

The Detroit Institute of Arts
Detroit, Michigan

Florence Museum
Florence, South Carolina

The Metropolitan Museum of Art
New York, New York

Museum of Fine Arts
Boston, Massachusetts

The Oriental Institute
The University of Chicago
Chicago, Illinois

Petrie Museum
University College London
London, England

Royal Ontario Museum
Toronto, Ontario, Canada

The University Museum
University of Pennsylvania
Philadelphia, Pennslyvania

TRAVEL SCHEDULE

McKissick Museum
The University of South Carolina
Columbia, South Carolina
April, 1988 to mid-June, 1988

Milwaukee Public Museum
Milwaukee, Wisconsin
July, 1988 to October, 1988

Denver Museum of Natural History
Denver, Colorado
late October, 1988 to mid-April, 1989

Los Angeles County Museum of
Natural History
Los Angeles, California
mid-May, 1989 to August, 1989

National Museum of Natural History
Smithsonian Institution
Washington, D.C.
late November, 1989 to late March, 1990

Since Napoleon and his grand army fought the enemy in the Nile Valley, the Western World has been fascinated with the power and splendor of the ancient kingdoms of the Pharaohs. Although many are familiar with the drama of spectacular excavations, the cracking of the linguistic mysteries through the Rosetta Stone, and Carter's discovery of the golden treasures from the tomb of Tutankhamon, we have yet to learn the complete story of ancient Egypt. Until now, no major exhibition has sought to tell the story of an earlier time, the Egypt before the first Pharaohs.

"The First Egyptians," a joint exhibition project undertaken by the University of South Carolina's McKissick Museum and the Earth Sciences and Resources Institute, explores ancient Egyptian civilization as interpreted through modern archaeology. Sponsored by the National Endowment for the Humanities, the exhibition focuses primarily on the cultural facets of early Egyptian society as it developed from small chiefdoms into the world's first nation-state between about 4000 B.C. and 2700 B.C. While past exhibitions have emphasized military glory, spectacular art and the monumental architecture of the Pharaohs, "The First Egyptians" examines the social, economic, technological and environmental factors that interacted to produce that extraordinary civilization. A second theme of the exhibition illustrates the procedures of the archaeologists, who through persistence, expertise and modern excavation techniques have recovered part of the significant information featured in this exhibition. Indeed, much of the recent information presented in this exhibition was unearthed by the

Sir William Matthew Flinders Petrie (1853-1942) Courtesy of The Petrie Museum, University College London, E. Neg. 1391.

THE FIRST EGYPTIANS: AN OVERVIEW

by Karin L. Willoughby
and
George D. Terry

Hierakonpolis Expedition, an interdisciplinary group of scholars that has been sponsored by the University of South Carolina since 1982.

This recently discovered information sheds light on some of the most significant cultural and artistic achievements in human history — the origins of towns, cities and centralized states; the development of organized warfare; monumental architecture; the advent of industry; the beginnings of a written language; the rise of kings and noblemen; and the creation of a system of values and beliefs that nourished the roots of ancient Egyptian culture a thousand years before the first Pharaoh.

Menes: The First Pharaoh

The ancient cultures explored in this exhibition evolved over the course of 2000 years and coalesced through a series of events that politically unified all of Egypt in about 3100 B.C. The evidence for these events and their cultural processes must be reconstructed from diverse clues ranging from early artistic representations and picture writing to, most importantly, the archaeological information unearthed from ancient villages, cities, temples, palaces and tombs.

One of the most important clues to the origins of Egyptian civilization is the Narmer Palette (see frontispiece), discovered at Hierakonpolis by a British expedition in 1897-98. This ceremonial artifact records several events commonly associated with Egypt's unification and provides an artistic and visual link between prehistory and history. Narmer is shown wearing two different crowns and his name is inscribed by both pictorial and phonetic means at the top of the Palette. The two crowns,

5

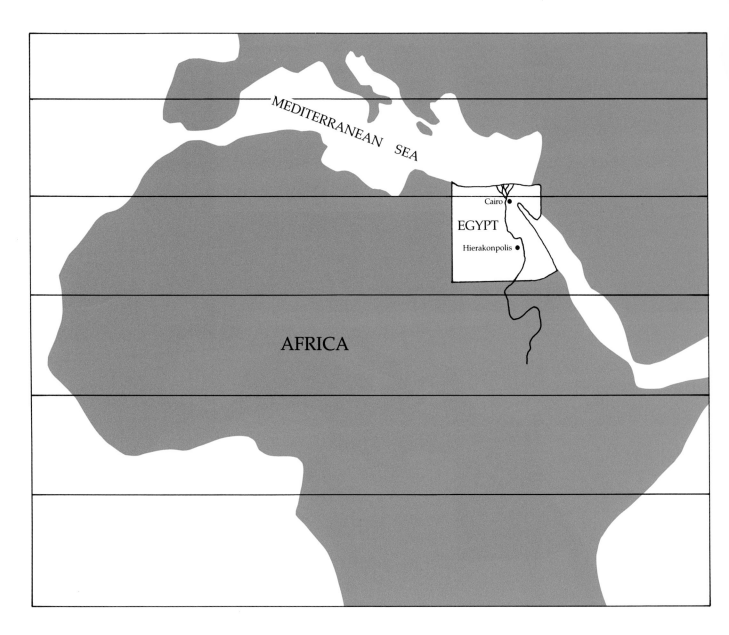

known as the white crown of Upper Egypt and the red crown of Lower Egypt, demonstrate the unification of the Egypts under the rule of one man. Furthermore, this man is named king by the presence of the symbol of the hawk-headed god Horus. Other symbols on the Palette show that force was used, probably both in battle and in ritual beheadings of defeated enemies. These and additional events, whether real or symbolic, are depicted on the Palette in a manner closely conforming to later writings that describe "Menes," the legendary first god-king of Egypt.

Appropriately, the emblem of "The First Egyptians" exhibition comes from the Narmer Palette. This symbol is comprised of two mythical animals that appear to be a mix of giraffes, serpents and lions that are carved in a "Mesopotamian" or "foreign" style that was generally abandoned by 2900 B.C.,

when pharaonic rule was firmly established and a purely Egyptian artistic style emerged. The two intertwined animal necks surround a circular depression that represents the original purpose of palettes — a place to grind and hold cosmetic powders. The entwined animals are thought to represent the unification and continued duality of Upper and Lower Egypt. As such, this unique symbol from Hierakonpolis expresses several of the themes of this exhibition — the continuity between Egyptian prehistory and history; the conceptual importance of "Tawy," the Two Lands, which is the ancient name for Egypt; the duality of Egypt's desert and river environments; and the momentous cultural processes that led to the unification of Upper and Lower Egypt. Finally, the Narmer Palette draws our attention to Hierakonpolis, where it was found. Ancient legends connect Hierakonpolis with the ancestors of the first Pharaohs and recent archaeological discoveries at the site are providing confirmation of these ancient tales.

Hierakonpolis (Hi-rah-kon'-po-lis)

Nekhen, now known as Hierakonpolis, the "City of the Hawk," was the ancient city located about 750 kilometers (450 miles) south of modern Cairo. Nekhen thrived from about 4000 B.C. to about 2230 B.C., and even then it was not completely abandoned. A temple to Horus the hawk-head god was carefully maintained there for another 2500 years. Several experts believe that Narmer was the king of Hierakonpolis when he conquered Lower Egypt. Whether he also conquered the rest of Upper Egypt or whether his immediate predecessors had already consolidated nearby territories is not yet understood. Several great kings, such as "Scorpion," are known from the period immediately preceding the earliest dynasties. Some experts refer to these rulers by the term Late Predynastic, while others use the phrase "Dynasty 0" or Protodynastic in recognition of the importance of these kings in consolidating Egypt. Whether Narmer is the last of the these kings or the first who ruled over a unified Egypt is not as important as the recognition that Nekhen was a large, wealthy, powerful community that successfully subdued her neighbors and imposed her cultural imprint on all of Egypt.

Hierakonpolis is the largest Predynastic site complex known in Egypt and encompasses the only known site of continual occupation from the herding camps of 4000 B.C., through the golden age of Nekhen with its thriving pottery industry, to the temple that still honored Horus at the time of the Greeks. These various communities expanded into the desert along the bed of a now dry stream, or wadi, that flowed 7000 to 5000 years ago.

The Hierakonpolis Expedition

The great discoveries at the turn of the century like the Narmer Palette and the Scorpion Macehead have been succeeded by the modern Hierakonpolis Expedition of the University of South Carolina, directed by Professor Michael Allen Hoffman. The Expedition was begun in 1967 by Professor Walter A. Fairservis as an interdisciplinary, regionally oriented attempt to trace the beginnings of Egyptian civilization.

Modern archaeological techniques recover kinds of data that were unrecognizable 50 years ago, data that permit a more complete reconstruction of these ancient communities. Even the best of the early archaeologists concentrated on recording and collecting whole objects. They did not sieve for broken pieces of pottery, plant seeds, or bits of animal bone. However, such information tells us about kiln sites, what plants were eaten, which animals were domesticated, as well as many other details of daily life. Furthermore, the technique of "reading the dirt" permits the recovery of architectural data. Turn-of-the-century archaeologists had little idea of what ancient Egyptian buildings looked like, unless the building was a well-preserved ruin. Careful examination of changes in soil color, composition, and texture allows modern workers to find mud walls, decayed wooden posts, old kilns and hearths and many other architectural details. This kind of information allows a much more complete picture of early Egyptian life than the earlier dependence on tomb finds.

Geography of Egypt

The modern country of Egypt lies just south of the Mediterranean Sea in the northeastern corner of Africa and shares borders with Libya, Sudan and Israel. While the borders of Egypt have frequently changed, the concept of Egypt as the northernmost country of the Nile Valley has existed for over 5000

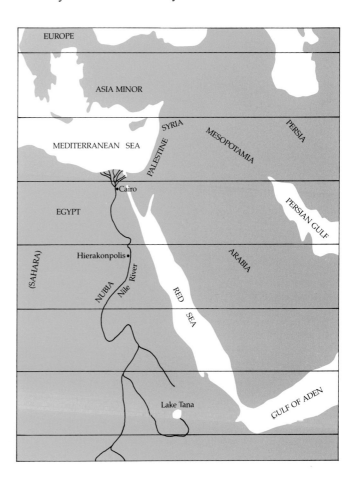

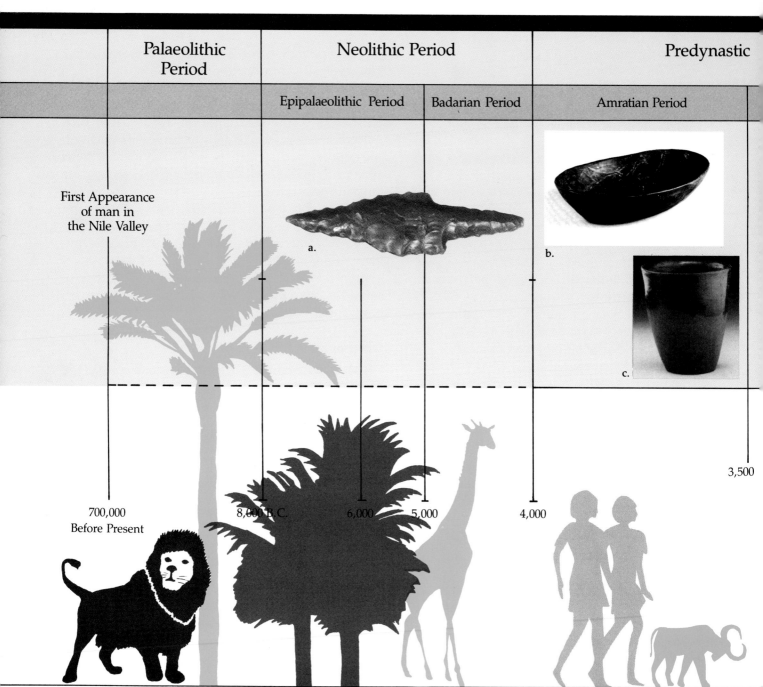

Palaeolithic Period	Neolithic Period		Predynastic
	Epipalaeolithic Period	Badarian Period	Amratian Period

First Appearance
of man in
the Nile Valley

a.

b.

c.

3,500

700,000
Before Present

8,000 B.C.

6,000

5,000

4,000

a. Stemmed Microlith Point; The Charleston Museum, South Carolina (ARM 311). b. Dish; Royal Ontario Museum, Toronto (900.2.103). c. Vase; ©1987 The Detroit Institute of Arts (79.441); Founders Society Purchase Acquisitions Fund. d. Jar; Royal Museum, Toronto (910.85.79) e. Stela; The Petrie

years. Capitals of Egypt have risen and fallen since the crucial joining of Upper and Lower Egypt at about 3100 B.C., but Egypt has remained. The ancient idea that Egypt is comprised of "Two Lands" or "Tawy" is not only a geographic reality but is also the environmental basis for Egyptian civilization. The Nile River even defined the seasons of the year for the ancient Egyptians — "flood," "coming forth" and "drought." Since the Nile River flows north, Upper Egypt is up-river or Southern Egypt and is generally considered to exist from the southern borders to the apex of the Nile Delta near Cairo. Upper Egypt is the Nile Valley while Lower Egypt is the Nile Delta which stretches from Cairo to the Mediterranean.

The change from desert to river valley can be so sudden that a person can stand with one foot in each environment. Recent archaeological work has shown that while the desert and the river are constants, the position of the border between them has varied a good deal. At the time of the flowering of pre-pharaonic cultures, northern Africa enjoyed a moister climate than at present. A few more inches of rain a year is all that is needed to greatly expand

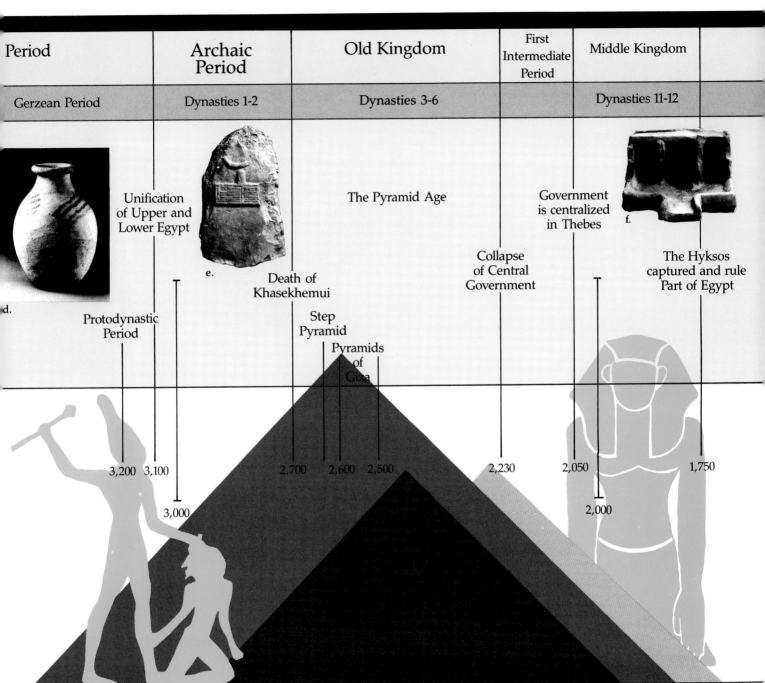

Museum, University College London (UC 14271). f. House Model; Gift of Egyptian Research Account; Museum of Fine Arts, Boston (07.551A). g. Statuette; Florence Museum, South Carolina (933).

the fertile areas of the Nile Valley such as at Hierakonpolis and in a large shallow valley known as the Fayum, near the Nile River Delta. The Great Wadi at Hierakonpolis ran through fields of green where today only desert exists. Thus, environmental change did affect the course of civilization in the Nile Valley.

Time and History in Egypt

This exhibition centers around the shift from prehistory to history and the unification of Egypt — a time represented by the Narmer Palette. A formal definition of history includes the idea that history has been recorded or written. The earliest inscriptions in Egypt predate the Narmer Palette, but are short and generally record a person's name, much as Narmer (translated as "Catfish") appears on the Palette. Thus, the start of "history" in Egypt is also recognizable as occurring at about the time of unification when judged by the development of writing. Scientists and Egyptologists have used many different means to develop the consensus that the forced union of Upper and Lower Egypt under the rule of Menes occurred at about 3100 B.C. A fuller

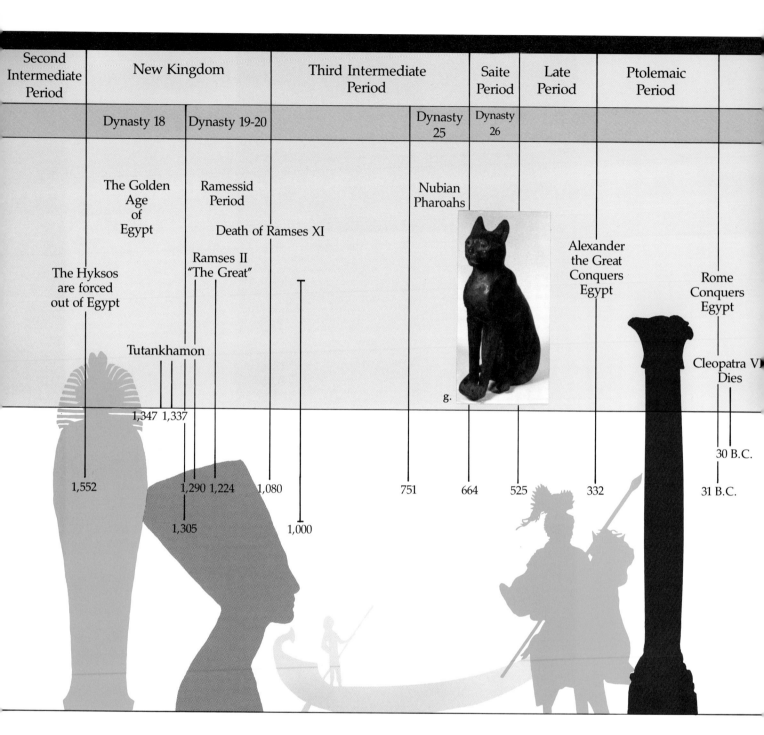

Second Intermediate Period	New Kingdom			Third Intermediate Period		Saite Period	Late Period	Ptolemaic Period	
	Dynasty 18	Dynasty 19-20			Dynasty 25	Dynasty 26			

The Golden Age of Egypt

Ramessid Period

Death of Ramses XI

Ramses II "The Great"

Nubian Pharoahs

The Hyksos are forced out of Egypt

Alexander the Great Conquers Egypt

Rome Conquers Egypt

Tutankhamon

Cleopatra VI Dies

g.

1,347 1,337

30 B.C.

1,552   1,290 1,224   1,080   751   664   525   332   31 B.C.

1,305   1,000

discussion of these issues is found in Dr. Hoffman's essay (p. 33).

The events leading to unification are considered prehistory, which is generally divided into Palaeolithic, Neolithic and Predynastic periods in Egypt, as can be seen on the introduction's timeline. The events after unification are historical and are divided into periods based on dynasties or "ruling families." Time periods after subjugation by Rome are not divided into dynasties.

Michael A. Hoffman's following essay on "Prelude to Civilization — The Predynastic Period in Egypt" discusses in detail events that occurred prior to unification and which are briefly reviewed here for easy reference to the timeline. The divisions of prehistoric time are based on economic and technological changes. Generally, Palaeolithic peoples hunted, gathered and fished, while Neolithic and Predynastic people farmed and herded as well. The Predynastic Period is further characterized by the development of permanent villages and towns and the start of early industries such as pottery-making and flint-knapping. The earliest successful mix of hunting and farming cultures in the Nile Valley is known as the Badarian Period, which existed from about 5500 to 3800 B.C. The emphasis on a varied assemblage of grave goods already existed by Badarian time.

The Amratian Period, which began about 3800 B.C. and ended by 3400 B.C., evolved directly from Badarian society. Settlements became larger and division of labor was needed in order to develop skills for the many tasks required to provide for the increasing population. The Gerzean Period, from about 3400 to 3200 B.C., developed directly from its Amratian roots in the Upper Nile Valley and was dominated by well-delineated social classes. Elaborate grave goods show that this culture focused on the creation, acquisition and enjoyment of material goods. By inference, the development of large grain stores also helped consolidate power in the hands of local chiefs and merchants. The Protodynastic Period, from about 3200 to 3100 B.C., developed directly from Gerzean society and formed the basis for the unification of Egypt.

The exhibition also briefly explores dynastic time and events in order to provide both a familiar historical basis and a useful perspective on the cultural elements of Predynastic time which formed the roots of Egyptian civilization. Dynasties have been grouped by later authorities into longer time periods in recognition of crucial events in Egyptian history and for easy reference. The first two dynasties are grouped as the Archaic Period (3100-2700 B.C.) and were the time of consolidation of Egypt under Pharaonic rule. Dr. Hoffman's essay reviews several events of Archaic time. The religious and artistic forms were formalized under the rule of the Pharaoh, who was himself a god. Authority became more and more centralized as local noblemen pledged fealty to regional lords who were pledged to the Pharaoh. Marriage and shared defense contracts cemented pharaonic gains, and the borders of Egypt were depopulated through war, capturing of prisoners and forced removal of local citizenry. Egypt was now set for its greatest era of political centralization.

The Old Kingdom started with the Third Dynasty and is better known as the "Age of Pyramids." From 2700 to 2230 B.C., art and architecture gave outward form to the height of Egyptian political centralization. After the last dynasty of the Old Kingdom, the political system became chaotic. No ruler was able to enforce his claim as Pharaoh until the rulers of the city of Thebes rose to power. This period, known as the Middle Kingdom, lasted from 2050 to 1750 B.C. Both internal conflicts and foreign aggression finally broke Thebes' hold on Egypt. No strong rulers appeared until 1552 B.C., when a series of Pharaohs from several families ruled Egypt. This New Kingdom Period included Egypt's "Golden Age;" the time of warrior kings such as Tuthmosis III; Ramesses II, Egypt's most famous monument builder; and relatively unimportant kings such as Tutankhamon.

With the death of the last Ramesses (the XI) in 1080 B.C., Egypt became prey to foreign rulers and reverted back into "the Two Lands." However, many of these foreign rulers assumed the forms of Egyptian government and adopted Egyptian art and customs. The Nubian and Libyan Pharaohs are two notable examples. The city of Sais produced the last native Egyptians who were able to rule as Pharaohs. From about 664 to 525 B.C., the Saite Period produced a cultural revival of Old Kingdom art forms. Politically, the Saites turned Egypt away from its African connections to become a Mediterranean power. When Alexander the Great conquered Egypt in 332 B.C. and the Ptolemies became Egypt's rulers, the ancient ways were ending. Although the Ptolemies adopted the outward forms of Egyptian culture, only Cleopatra VII was able to speak the Egyptian language. With her death in 30 B.C., Egypt turned to new sources for cultural expression.

Description of the Exhibition

The more than 130 objects in this exhibition have never been displayed together in the United States. These Egyptian artifacts were carefully selected to demonstrate the aesthetic skills of the early artists and craftsmen as well as to illustrate broader cultural themes.

The majority of artifacts presented in "The First Egyptians" were excavated from ancient cemeteries. These artifacts illustrate the importance the Egyptians placed on the burial rituals of the "mortuary cult," which was to play such a critical role in the political and social evolution of Egyptian civilization.

Among the spectacular array of objects chosen for the exhibition, several deserve special notice. From Abydos come artifacts representing kings of the First and Second Dynasties, including a gold-handled knife impressed with the name of King Djer on loan from the Royal Ontario Museum. Exquisitely carved stone and hand-thrown vases demonstrate the skills of the ancient craftsmen. From the "Main Deposit" at Hierakonpolis, discovered in 1898, comes an ivory figurine, alabaster bowls, sculpted animal statuettes and amulets. The artifacts from the "Main Deposit" provided some of the first clues that a rich culture existed in Egypt before the first Pharaohs — a culture that Dynastic Egyptians viewed with awe and respect. These artifacts are on loan from the Petrie Museum, University College London, and they provide important aesthetic and didactic components to the exhibition.

The exhibition artifacts are grouped to reinforce the social, political and spiritual values held by ancient Egyptians as well as to show chronological changes in artistic styles and developments in technology. One element of the archaeological methods portion of the show is a sequence of pots that three-dimensionally demonstrate the stylistic evolution of ceramic types as discovered by Sir Flinders Petrie (see "Evolution of Pottery Forms" p. 108 and Mrs. Adams' essay p. 47).

The exhibition is divided into four main topics. "The Search for Hierakonpolis" explores interdisciplinary techniques of modern archaeology. The earlier Egyptian expeditions conducted in the late nineteenth and early twentieth centuries by Quibell and Green, by Garstang and by Lansing are examined through archival photographs as well as through some of their finds. Modern techniques are highlighted through site photographs, a pottery group illustrating the Petrie Sequence and a model cross-section of Nehken. "The World of Ancient Egypt," the second topic area, presents a capsule review of time from the Palaeolithic Period to the 20th century. A timeline visually takes the visitor back through landmark events in Egypt from the Ptolemies (Cleopatra) to Predynastic time to provide a historical background for the exploration of Predynastic culture. "From Chiefs to Kings" looks at several elements of ancient Egypt — legitimization of power, creation of wealth, function of religion and the effects of a growing population. These ingredients of the world's first nation-state will be explored through artifacts that symbolize these ingredients. An Amratian tomb group and a representative Gerzean tomb group illustrate the artistic style and level of technological sophistication typical of these time periods while providing an opportunity to explore religious practices. Architectural elements recovered from Hierakonpolis are reviewed for cultural and population implications. Model reconstructions of an Amratian house and kiln, and the oldest known temple in Egypt (Gerzean age) conclude this area.

"'Tawy,' The Two Lands" reviews Hierakonpolis the Fayum, Naqada, Memphis, Abydos and Saq-qara, which were important Predynastic and Dynastic centers of activity or provinces. This final area also reviews the process of unification in terms of marriage, warfare and the closing of Egyptian borders to outsiders. The importance of the Nile in Ancient Egypt is stressed and the legend of Menes is explored.

Sir William Matthew Flinders Petrie

The "Father of Modern Egyptian Archaeology" was born in England in 1853. William Matthew Flinders Petrie was educated at home by his father, a chemist, surveyor and civil engineer; and his mother, a geologist. The wide range of subjects that the young Petrie studied led naturally to his first work as a surveyor. His interest in standards of measurement and an excellent field survey of Stonehenge prepared him for his first seasons in Egypt where he measured the Pyramids of Giza. Flinders Petrie then became active in the Egypt Exploration Fund (later Society) which would alternately fund and exasperate him. His own philosophy of digging was a radical departure from that of older archaeological treasure hunters, although he did not hesitate to collect "treasures." Petrie wrote "The true line lies as much in careful noting and comparison of small details as in more whole-sale and off-hand clearances." Although his techniques do not meet modern archaeological standards, his efforts to record accurately were advanced for his time. His theories were not always well thought out, but his data continue to be invaluable. William Matthew Flinders Petrie was knighted in 1923 for his many discoveries and for his efforts to disseminate his knowledge through teaching and publication.

Objects in this exhibition strongly reflect Petrie's prodigious efforts. Artifacts from Sir Flinders' personal collections at The Petrie Museum, University College London are exhibited next to Exploration Fund pieces from The Charleston Museum and The University Museum at The University of Pennsylvania.

**Importance of Pottery
in Reconstructing Ancient Egypt**

One of Petrie's most significant contributions to Egyptian archaeology is a method he termed Sequence Dating. This method permits the chronological or sequential dating of artifacts, especially pots, by comparison of styles of decoration. Petrie developed a chart summarizing the evolution of Predynastic pottery and other artifacts from oldest to youngest. The history of Petrie's system, its recent revisions and its relevance to the study of

Excavating in Egypt, Professor Petrie at Thebes, by Henry Wallis. Courtesy of The Petrie Museum, University College London, E. Neg. 2225.

Predynastic cultures are discussed in detail in the essay by Mrs. Barbara Adams on "Predynastic Pottery" (p. 47).

The value of Petrie's method cannot be overestimated. Few prehistoric artifacts carry a date of manufacture and a method to recognize which object is older or younger is essential for unravelling the relative age of these artifacts. Sir Flinders Petrie's method is still used today despite recent developments in other chronological methods such as radiometric dating. Petrie's recognition of changing artistic and technological styles permitted the development of the Predynastic chronology discussed in Dr. Hoffman's essay. Sequence Dating also directly links Predynastic Egypt to the era of the Pharaohs, thereby giving us an insight into the emerging Egyptian civilization.

Who, Then, Were "The First Egyptians"?

Within the context of this exhibition, the first Egyptians are the indigenous people of the Nile Valley who developed the distinctive culture of ancient Egypt or "Tawy" between 5000 and 3100 B.C. These Egyptians were an intermingling of Nile Valley Palaeolithic descendents and repeated influxes of Northern African, Eastern Mediterranean and Sudanese peoples.

By 3100 B.C., Upper and Lower Egyptians displayed a range of physical features, although most were short to medium height by American standards. Their skin tones varied from light brown to black and they had straight to curly brown or black hair. If there were any recognizable trends in features, the northern Egyptians had a greater component of Mediterranean characteristics, while their southern countrymen had darker skins, curly hair and other features in common with their Nubian neighbors.

Obviously, unification occurred over a period of years, perhaps over generations, and it has not been proven beyond doubt that one man took all the decisive actions needed to produce a united Egypt. When "Menes" first proclaimed himself god as well as king, the culture of Egyptian civilization was already in existence. The Predynastic culture of Upper Egypt, superimposed on that of Lower Egypt, produced a people who used recognizable artistic, social, religious and political forms for 3,000 years.

No exhibition before "The First Egyptians" has ever attempted to integrate the several cultural developments of prehistoric Egypt that were essential to the fabric and form of the Egypt of the Pharaohs. Such a comprehensive overview requires insight into several facets of human endeavor in the Nile Valley that have been only recently recovered. The data and interpretations of events at the archaeological site of Hierakonpolis have served as a microcosm for this review of important cultural benchmarks of ancient Egyptian civilization.

Hierakonpolis is the only known site in Egypt that was occupied continually during the critical time period of 4000 B.C. through the height of political centralization achieved during Old Kingdom time. The importance of Hierakonpolis to the ancient Egyptians has long been known from pyramid inscriptions and legends. However, the essential role of the city in both the creation and cultural development of ancient Egypt is only now being understood as new archaeological finds document everyday life, developing industry, extensive trade, architectural style, religious practices, artistic forms and political power.

"The First Egyptians" explores the development of these essential cultural elements from about 4000 B.C. to about 3000 B.C. During this time, Egyptian civilization grew from herding camps and farming villages to the world's first nation-state and set the framework of Egyptian culture for 3000 years.

32. Jar; Late Gerzean; The University Museum, University of Pennsylvania (E-1395).

THE FIRST
EGYPTIANS

7. Double Jar; Amratian; Royal Ontario Museum, Toronto (900.2.11).

11. Basalt Jar with two narrow string-hole handles from el'Adaima; Ht: 28.9 cm; The Brooklyn Museum, (07.447.187); Museum Collection Fund.

14. Jar; Late Amratian-Gerzean; The University Museum of The University of Pennsylvania (E-14383).

19. Hanging Vase; Gerzean; Royal Ontario Museum, Toronto (908.40.1).

21. Vessel; Gerzean; Courtesy of The Oriental Institute of The University of Chicago (OIM 29874) (P.67660/N.46436).

25. Roll Rim Jar; Middle Gerzean; The Petrie Museum, University College London (UC 6340).

28. Jar; Middle Gerzean; The Petrie Museum, University College London (UC 10702).

33. Red-polished Jar; Late Gerzean-early Protodynastic (Late Naqada II-early Naqada III); From el'Ma'mariya; Ht: 25.9 cm; The Brooklyn Museum, (07.477.349); Museum Collection Fund.

37. Frog-Shaped Vase; Gerzean-Protodynastic; Royal Ontario Museum, Toronto (910.100.3).

40. Serpentine jar with two wavy handles; Protodynastic (Naqada III); from Abu Zaiden; Ht: 14.1 cm; The Brooklyn Museum, (09.889.31); Museum Collection Fund.

53. Saucer of pink limestone with horizontal rim; Early Dynasty I; Ht: 2.8 cm, Diam: 11.0 cm; The Brooklyn Museum, (09.889.29); Museum Collection Fund.

54. Bowl; Dynasties XI or XII, Nubian C (Middle Kingdom); Royal Ontario Museum, Toronto (900.2.91).

60. Disk Macehead; Amratian-early Gerzean (Naqada I-early Naqada II); From el'Adaima; Ht: 2.4 cm, Diam: 9.1 cm; The Brooklyn Museum, (07.447.873); Museum Collection Fund.

68. Schist Palette; Gerzean-Protodynastic (Naqada II-Naqada III), from Geblein (?); Lth: 29.5 cm. The Brooklyn Museum (16.580.126); Gift of the Estate of Charles Edwin Wilbour through Mrs. Evangeline Wilbour Blashfield.

67. House Model; Gerzean; Royal Ontario Museum, Toronto (900.2.45).

91. House Model; Dynasty XII (Middle Kingdom); Gift of Egyptian Research Account; Museum of Fine Arts, Boston (07.551A)

123. Knife impressed with Horus Banner and Hieroglyphs of King Djer; Dynasty I (Archaic); Royal Ontario Museum, Toronto (914.3).

In 1894 William Matthews Flinders Petrie, the father of modern archaeology in Egypt, began excavations at Naqada, just north of Luxor. His discoveries radically changed existing theories of Egypt's past. At Naqada, Petrie found a huge cemetery containing over 2,100 simple rectangular tombs. At first, he was unable to date them because of their unfamiliar style and contents. The bodies of the deceased were lain in a flexed or contracted position and were accompanied by large numbers of handmade pots, green slate pigment palettes, ivory and bone pendants and combs, fancy flint knives, terra cotta figurines and a rich array of stone and shell beads. Petrie soon realized that these graves and the objects in them belonged to a hitherto unknown pre-pharaonic culture which he christened "Predynastic."

The Predynastic era was typified by a mixed subsistence economy of farming, herding and fishing; the growth of villages and towns; semi-industrial pottery manufacture; warfare; rich cemeteries; complex art; interregional and, eventually, international trade; the beginnings of monumental public architecture, including large temple complexes; and increasingly complex social stratification. Predynastic culture (often called the "Naqada Culture") originated in the Nile Valley within a 650 kilometer (390 mile) stretch of the river between the city of Assiut in Middle Egypt and the Second Cataract of the Nile in the northern Sudan (Lower Nubia). After about 3500 B.C., it spread northward where it appears at Minshat Abu Omar in the eastern Delta by Gerzean (3500-3200 B.C.) times.

Sorting potsherds at Hierakonpolis.

PRELUDE TO CIVILIZATION: THE PREDYNASTIC PERIOD IN EGYPT

by Michael Allen Hoffman

The origin of the Predynastic culture is still a matter of heated debate among specialists. The most educated guesses suggest that this spectacular culture originated sometime between about 5500 and 4000 B.C. from the fusion of desert herding and farming peoples with Nilotic fishing, hunting and gathering folk.

The Search for the Origins of Egyptian Civilization

Despite the discoveries of Petrie and his successors, the idea that the impressive achievements of Egyptian civilization could have developed normally from prehistoric roots without significant foreign influence has been difficult for many to accept. For most, ancient Egypt is defined by the soaring pyramids, massive temples, mysterious mummies and extraordinary art of Pharaonic times. The search for the origins of Egyptian civilization — for the first Egyptians — has long been the subject of academic debate and popular interest, most of it sober, some of it outrageous. In the last two decades the focus has shifted from the armchair back to the field, where there has been a resurgence of new archaeological excavations in settlement sites like Hierakonpolis. The patient application of modern scientific techniques has yielded discoveries which allow us to trace Egypt's cultural origins directly by establishing an unbroken succession of social and economic development linking Pharaonic Egypt to its Predynastic past.

The purpose of this essay is to provide a fresh view of the evolution of Egyptian civilization from the Predynastic Period (ca. 4000-3100 B.C.) into the first two dynasties of "Archaic" times (ca. 3100-2700

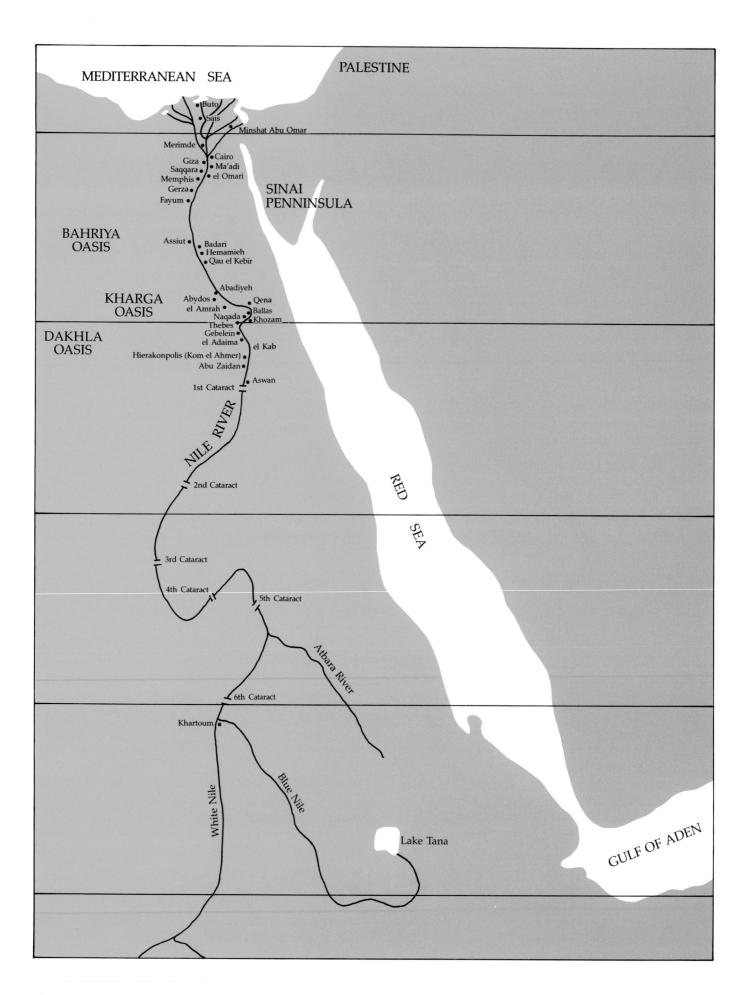

MEDITERRANEAN SEA

PALESTINE

Buto
Sais
Minshat Abu Omar

Merimde

Giza
Saqqara
Memphis
Gerza
Fayum

Cairo
Ma'adi
el Omari

SINAI
PENNINSULA

BAHRIYA
OASIS

Assiut
Badari
Hemamieh
Qau el Kebir

Abadiyeh

KHARGA
OASIS

Abydos
el Amrah
Naqada
Thebes
Gebelein
el Adaima
Hierakonpolis (Kom el Ahmer)
Abu Zaidan

Qena
Ballas
Khozam

el Kab

DAKHLA
OASIS

Aswan

1st Cataract

NILE RIVER

2nd Cataract

RED
SEA

3rd Cataract

4th Cataract

5th Cataract

Atbara River

6th Cataract

Khartoum

White Nile

Blue Nile

Lake Tana

GULF OF ADEN

B.C.). By choice, the focal point of this discussion, as with the exhibition "The First Egyptians," is the Predynastic Period. Because it is now clear that Predynastic culture was a direct ancestor of early Pharaonic civilization, it is useful to draw cultural parallels between the two periods.

Before reviewing the chronology, environment and cultural development of Predynastic Egypt based on the contributions of new archaeological research, the significance of this period for world prehistory needs to be considered in light of the broader issues of human social evolution. Studying anew the origins of ancient Egyptian civilization has a special relevance for modern man because it offers an explanation for one of the oldest and most vexing questions in human history — how and why did the world's complex societies evolve? Although prehistory may reach back four to five million years, mankind has lived in nation-states (large, centrally governed geographical areas) for only about five thousand years — a mere 1/1000th of that period.

At the end of the Pleistocene era (ca. 8000 B.C.) most of our ancestors hunted, fished and gathered wild plants to survive. Settlements were generally small, seasonal camps inhabited by two or three families, totaling twenty or thirty people. Social differences were minimal and based primarily on age and sex. Leaders and shamans accumulated no wealth nor could they pass on their authority. The introduction of domesticated plants and animals (at different times in different areas of the world) changed all this by allowing a rapid increase in population and an accumulation of wealth and power. At first, camps grew into permanent villages; soon towns of a few hundred swelled to cities of thousands. The division of labor became more complex as fulltime craftsmen and artisans (potters, woodcarvers, metal workers, traders) and early rulers — chiefs and priests — appeared. Wealth and power were accumulated and passed on within families.

Out of this milieu, the world's six original independent civilizations arose — Mesopotamia, Egypt, the Indus Valley, China, Mesoamerica and Peru. Of these early complex societies, Egypt provides the first and only example of a politically centralized nation-state. When, where, how and why did such an extraordinary social revolution occur? "The First Egyptians" exhibition explores these questions visually while this essay considers some of the related issues in light of past discoveries and ongoing research.

Chronology

To understand the origins and development of Egyptian civilization, we must be able to arrange events of the past in their correct order. Because the rise of the ancient Egyptian state spans both prehistory and history, dating this time period involves methods and techniques from two very different fields.

Egyptian prehistory, the time before writing, is generally divided on the basis of major stylistic, technological and economic changes such as methods for manufacturing stone tools, the use of pottery and the appearance of agriculture. Ancient Egyptian history is broken down into 32 dynasties or ruling houses, based on a chronological scheme devised by the priest Manetho (Table 1). Manetho, a native Egyptian, wrote a condensed history of his country for its Macedonian ruler Ptolemy II about 280 B.C., drawing on ancient lists of kings preserved on papyrus rolls and engraved on temple walls. Manetho wrote in Greek — the international scientific language of his day — but must have found his task difficult because of the fundamental differences between ancient Egyptian and Greek approaches to history. Since the time of Thucydides in the late fifth century B.C., Greek authors had striven to write history in terms of cause and effect — a method which underlies all modern historiography and social sciences. This method contrasts radically with the ancient Egyptian approach that stressed the central and mystical role of the divine Pharaoh as a champion of timeless traditional values. The history of Egypt produced by Manetho was little more than a chronicle of idealized events, arranged from youngest to oldest, according to the reign of a particular king.

Until the turn of the century, we possessed no concrete evidence for Manetho's first two dynasties. Then Flinders Petrie excavated the tombs of Egypt's first monarchs at Abydos. Petrie recovered all the tombs of the First Dynasty kings (ca. 3100-2900 B.C.) plus the tombs of Peribsen and Khasekhemui from late in the Second Dynasty (ca. 2900-2700 B.C.). Petrie also found some tombs belonging to local late Predynastic or "Protodynastic" rulers, such as Ka and Irj-Hor. "The First Egyptians" has brought together a number of rare items inscribed with the names of Egypt's first rulers from these tombs. The finds at Abydos not only support Manetho's chronology and illustrate the material culture of earliest Dynastic times, but clearly showed connections to the preceding Predynastic epoch. Despite its limitations and errors, Manetho's work continues to

Mapping and surveying at Hierakonpolis.

provide historians with a useful chronological framework.

In Egypt, the line between history and prehistory is drawn at the very beginning of the First Dynasty (ca. 3100 B.C.) and marked by the first evidence of hieroglyphic writing. This is an arbitrary division, since the origin of writing probably dates back several centuries into the Predynastic and since the earliest historical inscriptions (such as those on the Narmer Palette) are short and of limited use. There are two principal prehistoric epochs — the Palaeolithic and Predynastic. Generally speaking, Palaeolithic peoples hunted, foraged and fished, while Predynastic peoples practiced agriculture and herding. The names used to characterize different periods within the Palaeolithic era reflect a simple separation into Lower, Middle and Late, while Predynastic divisions generally derive from the names of particular archaeological sites, such as Badari, Amrah, Gerzeh and Naqada. The Palaeolithic actually began as early as 4 or 5 million years ago in southern and eastern Africa, but the earliest evidence for man's presence in Egypt dates back about 700,000 years. Typical Palaeolithic cultural remains are found until about 8,000 years ago. The Predynastic, by contrast, began shortly before 4000 B.C. and ended with political unification under the first kings of the First Dynasty about 3100 B.C. Today, the Predynastic is usually divided into the following periods: Badarian (ca. 5500/4000-3800 B.C.), Amratian (Naqada I) (ca. 3800-3500/3400

B.C.), Gerzean (Naqada II) (ca. 3500/3400-3200 B.C.) and Protodynastic (Naqada III) (ca. 3200-3100 B.C.) (See Figure 2). The gap between Late Palaeolithic and early Predynastic (ca. 8000-6000 B.C. to ca. 4000 B.C.) was a time of transition from hunting and gathering to farming cultures and is still poorly known. Archaeologists use the term "Epipalaeolithic" to designate the last Palaeolithic cultures (ca. 8000-5000 B.C.), such as the "el Kabien" of Upper Egypt, and "Neolithic" (ca. 6000-4000 B.C.) to identify the first farming communities of the Nile Valley.

Archaeologists rely on several chronological methods — relative dating, cross-dating and radiometric dating — to tie artifacts and cultures to our own calendar. Relative dating determines the age of two or more objects or events in relation to one another. The most useful relative chronological tool for Predynastic research is Petrie's "Sequence Dating," developed originally to date the graves at Naqada. Sequence Dating arranges different classes of artifacts in stylistic sequences from oldest to youngest and is discussed in detail in Mrs. Adams' essay (p. 47). Cross-dating compares objects to similar pieces found in datable contexts at other sites. For example, certain types of pottery found in Predynastic sites come from Palestine where they are known to occur in Chalcolithic (Copper Age) or Early Bronze Age levels of tells (settlement mounds composed of superimposed layer cake-like strata of debris). Such stratified sites are rare in Egypt —

although not nearly as rare as many archaeologists believe — and require special skills to dig properly. Prior to 1984 only one Predynastic site, the small hamlet of Hemamieh excavated by Gertrude Caton-Thompson in 1924, yielded a well-stratified succession of (broken) Predynastic pottery. Regrettably, the Predynastic sequence was incomplete because Hemamieh was abandoned well before the end of the Predynastic. Not until 1984 did excavations at Hierakonpolis reveal a sequence connecting Predynastic and Dynastic levels in a manner comparable to the famous stratified tells of Palestine. The discoveries at Hierakonpolis open up the possibility of scientifically cross-dating Predynastic sites all over Egypt.

In the last forty years, the technique of radiocarbon or carbon 14 dating has grown in popularity. Theoretically, the method allows us to date organic material such as wood, shell or bone based on the known "half-life" decay rate of the unstable isotope C-14. The length of time it takes for half the original amount of C-14 to decay to nitrogen is known as its "half-life." Although this method produces an estimate that can be related to our own calendar, there is a certain amount of built-in imprecision so that the date is usually written 3500 ± 100 years B.P. (Before Present). Recently, a correction factor has been introduced based on correlation with tree rings. Unfortunately, even with this safeguard, dates from the Predynastic are subject to heliomagnetic anomalies, popularly called "wiggles," which might distort a seemingly accurate series of readings by several hundred years. Given such difficulties, it is nothing short of astonishing that both historians working backwards in time from their Dynastic dates and prehistorians using radiocarbon estimates are able to agree on a date of about 3100 B.C. (± 100 years) for the end of the last Predynastic period and the beginning of the First Dynasty (i.e., the time of Narmer).

Sites like Hierakonpolis allow us to combine different dating techniques to build a chronological framework within which historians and prehistorians can study the origins of Egypt's precocious civilization.

Environment

The geographical divisions of Egypt — both ancient and modern — provide spatial starting points for understanding the environment in which Egyptian civilization evolved in much the same way that Manetho's chronology, Petrie's Sequence Dates and modern carbon 14 dating give us a framework for studying change through time. Ancient Egyp-

tians conceived of their country as "Tawy," the Two Lands. Upper or southern Egypt comprised the Nile Valley from Aswan to roughly the site of modern Cairo. Lower or northern Egypt consisted of the river's delta from its apex at Cairo to the Mediterranean coast.

Egypt's unity arose from the life-giving Nile, while the geographical and cultural divisions implicit in the terms Upper and Lower Egypt were likewise products of cultural and ecological differences created by the river and climate. On the one hand there was the fertile alluvial black land or "Kemet," which contrasted strikingly with the barren desert frontiers, the red land or "Deshru." The tension created between these two environments, and the cultures they spawned, dominated both Egyptian prehistory and history for thousands of years.

The ancient Greek geographer Herodotus, writing about 450 B.C., noted the importance of the river

TABLE I Dynastic Chronology of Ancient Egypt

Period Name	Absolute Date (B.C.)	Dynasty
Archaic	3100-2700	I AND II
Old Kingdom	2700-2230	III-VI
First Intermediate Period	2230-2130	VII-X
Middle Kingdom	2050-1750	XI-XII
Second Intermediate Period	1750-1552	XIII-XVII
New Kingdom	1552-1080	XVIII-XX
Third Intermediate Period	1080-664	XXI-XXV
Saite Period	664-525	XXVI
Late Period	525-332	XXVII-XXXI
Ptolemaic	332(323)-31	XXXII

TABLE II Predynastic Chronology of Ancient Egypt

Date (B.C.)	Upper Egypt	Lower Egypt
3100	Protodynastic	Protodynastic
3300	Late Gerzean (Naqada II)	Late Gerzean/ Maadian
3500	Early Gerzean (Naqada II)	Omari B?
4000	Amratian (Naqada I)	Omari A?
5000	Badarian	Merimden/Fayum A
(5500 ?)		

Nile for Egypt's unparalleled wealth. Without the Nile, virtually all Egypt would be desert. The rich black soils deposited by its annual floods made it one of the great granaries of the ancient world. Those yearly inundations — the result of monsoon rains falling on the far-off Ethiopian highlands and filling Lake Tana — were both the source of Egypt's wealth and the cause of its greatest perils. If the river ran too high or too low, famine and chaos stalked the land. The long, easily navigated course of the Nile also became a highway for commerce, people and ideas which flowed between Africa and the Middle Eastern and Mediterranean lands.

The Nile's waters derive principally from two rivers — the Blue Nile, which starts at Lake Tana and provides 80 percent of the Nile's volume, and the White Nile, whose source is Lake Victoria in Uganda. These two streams join at the city of Khartoum in the Sudan. The Atbara is the only other tributary to contribute even a trickle to the mighty Nile as it courses toward the sea.

In the past, the Sudanic rain belt has temporarily shifted north, radically transforming the Sahara. In a naturally arid land like Egypt, even a minute increase in precipitation brings about a rapid alteration of the total ecosystem. Such changes have occurred several times in Egyptian prehistory with important consequences for human culture. Climatologists, botanists, zoologists and archaeologists have undertaken research which allows us to reconstruct several of the important rainy periods in northeastern Africa during the last 300,000 or more years. Major rainy periods or "pluvials" have had significant impact on the Hierakonpolis region, causing the desert to bloom and allowing settlements to extend further into the desert than they do today.

The last pluvial (7000-2500 B.C.) is the most important for Predynastic development. It created a special set of environmental conditions which triggered the settlement of the newly verdant Saharan grasslands and the rapid adoption of herding and farming strategies by the colonists. Most experts now believe that food production and animal domestication originated in the Middle East and quickly spread into northern Africa around 6000 B.C.

Almost certainly the new way of life originated as a trickle of people and ideas rather than as a flood of immigrants. Soon indigenous peoples adopted many of the cultivated plants and domesticated animals. New subsistence strategies began to subtly change social groups. Innovations were especially welcome among the colonists of the Sahara, who were sensitive to exploiting a newly available habitat and aware of the advantages a fresh economic strategy could produce. To the Middle Eastern domesticates, Saharan peoples added a strong emphasis on cattle pastoralism that was later echoed in the political and religious symbolism of pharaonic Egypt and other African cultures.

Early Neolithic Cultures of Egypt and the Sudan

Ironically, the Neolithic life style did not spread to the middle and upper Egyptian Nile Valley for some time. Between 6000 and 5000 B.C., herding and horticulture appeared throughout Egypt's Western Desert, where it has been noted at Kharga and Dakhla Oases, Nabta Playa, Bir Terfawi, Selima, the Gebel Uweinat and Gilf Kebir as well as at hundreds of localities in the central and western Sahara. Neolithic culture also spread very early into the Delta, Fayum and the Sudan. Conclusive evidence is found in the Delta from Merimde in the West, at Buto, the northern counterpart of Hierakonpolis, and has just been detected at Minshat Abu Omar in the East. Doubtless, hundreds of other "northern Predynastic" or Neolithic sites still lie beneath the Delta's deep alluvium. Another later Neolithic tradition, identified just south of Cairo, at Maadi and Omari, shows trade links to the Upper Egyptian Predynastic and Palestinian communities but continued to maintain cultural diversity into Early Dynastic times. An early Neolithic tradition has long been known in the Fayum, but new research by Polish and American teams has shed light on its highly localized lacustrine orientation. Finally, an early food-producing tradition at Nilotic Sudanese sites like Khartoum precedes any of the classic Predynastic developments further north.

Between 5500 and 4000 B.C., rainfall grew more erratic and lakes and streams dried up while the population continued to grow. The increased need for food forced pastoral and horticultural peoples north, and some settled in the central and southern Egyptian Nile Valley. In mixing with or displacing indigenous food gatherers, these Neolithic peoples laid the foundations for the earliest Upper Egyptian Predynastic culture — the Badarian. Ultimately, the Pharaonic civilization arose from Badarian culture.

The Badarian Period

As yet we have no direct evidence of the indigenous ancestry of Badarian culture. Recent discoveries by a Polish expedition at Gebel Tarif near the Valley of the Kings suggest the kind of primitive Neolithic society from which the Badarian probably

An excavated grid revealing ancient walls and post holes.

evolved. Unsubstantiated reports from the Eastern Desert and finds in the Sudan at sites like Kadada suggest similarities with early Badarian flaring rimmed, zoned incised beakers once called "Tasian." Still, the search for Badarian origins remains one of the great unsolved mysteries of Egyptian archaeology.

Generally, we date the beginning of the Badarian Period sometime between 5500 and 4000 B.C. and its end about 3800 B.C. The Badarian seems to have developed in central Egypt between the modern cities of Assiut and Tahta about 350 kilometers (210 miles) south of Cairo. Although this is assumed to be the Badarian heartland, it may simply be that accidents of discovery and preservation have biased our sample, so that when other regions are better explored the core area of the Badarian might be extended. Already, typical Badarian-like "rippled" pottery has been noted in several localities at Hierakonpolis and el Kab, 270 kilometers (160 miles) south of the type site of el Badari.

The Badarian, like later Predynastic cultures, showed a tendency toward ornamentation and an emphasis on the burial of rich grave goods in simple oval tombs — traits which distinguished it from contemporaneous groups in the Western Desert and the Delta, but which it apparently shared with its Sudanic Nubian counterparts. Its pottery was thin, well-made and characterized by a refined rippled and black-topped, plum red burnished decoration. Simple oval and rectangular palettes often bear traces of red ocher or malachite green on their surfaces, while pots have been found filled with pigment. Their beautiful hollow-based arrowheads are also found in northern and desert Neolithic sites and suggest some contact during the period 5000-4000 B.C. Countless necklaces and belts of shell, ivory, carnelian, glazed steatite, jasper and occasionally copper, were buried with the dead, as were well-made ivory spoons and combs, strange humanoid terracotta figurines, animal amulets and even carved wooden throwing sticks used in the hunt. Often, the shells were from the Red Sea and may have been used as a medium of exchange. A few graves contained small copper borers and pins which were apparently hammered or anviled rather than cast as in the Middle East and eastern Europe. The presence of copper artifacts has led many prehistorians to classify the Badarian as a "Chalcolithic" or Copper Age culture. We should not place too much emphasis on its primitive metallurgy, since chipped stone (flint) tools such as bifacial sickle blades, push planers, non-bifacial endscrapers and perforators, as well as groundstone artifacts, including axes and crude basalt vases, dominated the technology. The presence of clay boat models in tombs reminds us that Badarians already plied the Nile and enjoyed a mobility and ease of transport that helped unify the Upper Egyptian Predynastic cultures.

Badarian clothing was made from both tanned leather and extremely fine linen. Fine baskets and mats were woven, and cultivated crops included wheat and barley for food and flax for linen. It is doubtful whether irrigation was employed. Domesticated animals included the familiar sheep, goats, cattle and pigs.

Unfortunately, we know little of Badarian settlements. Architecture was apparently in wood and mud-plastered reed, but turn-of-the-century excavation techniques were generally not geared to recovering such evidence nor to examining ancient settlement and community plans. Although comparatively modest by later Predynastic standards, Badarian tombs show differences in the quality and number of exotic grave goods that already reflect a society stratified by differences in wealth and status. There is good reason to believe that local chiefdoms existed and that the mortuary cult had become a critical focal point for marshalling and displaying wealth, legitimizing authority and communicating religious beliefs. Not coincidentally, the time-honored practice of tomb robbery seems to have originated during the Badarian.

The Amratian or Naqada I Period

The Amratian Period developed directly from Badarian roots, as is proven by striking similarities in artifacts such as black-topped plum red ware pottery, slate pigment palettes and ivory combs; the persistence of distinctive burial practices; and stratigraphic continuity between the two periods at both Hemamieh and Hierakonpolis. What remains unclear is whether and to what degree non-Badarian cultures might have contributed to the Amratian.

Numerous radiocarbon estimates suggest that the Amratian began somewhere between 3800 and 3700 B.C. and lasted until about 3500 to 3400 B.C. Characteristic Amratian "white cross-lined" painted and black-topped pottery is distributed widely throughout the Nile Valley from just 30 kilometers (20 miles) south of Aswan at Bahan to the Badari

district in the North, a distance of approximately 375 kilometers (225 miles) as the crow flies. The similarity of artifacts over such an extensive area is explained by the efficiency of river transport. Although the succeeding Gerzean or Naqada II Period is famous for its representations of boats on rocks, pottery and tomb walls, we often ignore the widespread paintings of river craft on Amratian pots.

Another major factor that contributed to the spread of Amratian culture is the distinctive Predynastic death cult, which originated in the Badarian. Generally, Amratian tombs are larger and more richly furnished than their predecessors and reflect clear differences in wealth and status. Recent excavations at Hierakonpolis have shown that large, late Amratian tombs already had their own special precinct in a cemetery. One of these tombs, the largest of its era yet found in Egypt, measured 2.9 meters (9.5 feet) long by 1.6 meters (5.2 feet) wide and 1.5 meters (4.9 feet) deep. While Badarian tombs were simply stocked, Amratian graves often held twenty or thirty vessels, including storage jars, red burnished and decorated bowls; a variety of black-topped vases and beakers; lozenge- or diamond-shaped slate palettes; occasional copper ornaments; well-made bifacial flint lanceheads; bone and ivory combs, pendants and amulets; increasingly well-made stone vases (still primarily in basalt); stone and shell beads; painted reed arrows tipped with fine chisel-shaped flint points; and beautifully ground, polished, green and white porphyry disc-shaped maceheads. These latter objects are important because they are the first identifiable "powerfacts" or physical symbols of power. In ancient Egypt, as in more recent Western societies, maceheads were symbols of royal power and legitimate authority as well as of the king's prowess as a war leader. Historic Egyptian kings from Narmer to the Ptolemies — a period of over 3,000 years — were depicted wielding their maceheads against the heads of hapless enemies. Evidence from settlement excavations and detailed regional surveys at Hierakonpolis prove that the production of maceheads, pottery and probably many other items used in the mortuary cult and in everyday life, was highly organized on a proto-industrial scale. It now seems likely that "mortuary kits" of pottery, slate palettes, maceheads, ivory pins and other jewelry were exported up and down the Nile from major centers like Hierakonpolis. The discovery of the first kilns for producing the fancy Plum Red Ware pottery adjacent to an elite Amra-

Recording finds on site at Hierakonpolis.

tian cemetery further suggests the relationship between the growth of the powerful elite and the production of fancy items for the mortuary cult.

Extensive evidence from Hierakonpolis also reflects the size, variety and extent of Amratian settlements. Two centers of settlement dominated the landscape from 3800 B.C. to 3500 B.C. Each included zones for habitation, industry and trash disposal. Surrounding the two centers were smaller farming hamlets, herders' camps, cemeteries and holy places. Dwellings ranged from small, circular huts in seasonal camps to more substantial, rectangular houses of mudbrick and wattle-and-daub in the towns. The wattle-and-daub houses, in which mud is plastered over a woven wood and reed framework, often had floors dug below ground level.

Houses were sometimes bunched close together and sometimes surrounded by spacious, fenced enclosures. These dwellings, and the different, often specialized objects found in them, reflect underlying economic and social differences in the community that herald the eventual emergence of the politically powerful elite.

The area covered by the housing sites — some 100 acres — suggests that during the Amratian, or Naqada I, the regional population of Hierakonpolis had soared from several hundred people to several thousand — between 2,300 and 10,500. Such large populations were essential to the development of a state.

Ethnographic studies of historic societies with subsistence strategies and material cultures comparable to the Amratian, suggest that when the population size reaches a few thousand, the area governed extends well beyond a single community. Viewed in another way, the region needed to support the large and concentrated population of late Amratian Hierakonpolis must have extended well beyond the 10-kilometer (6-mile) stretch of Nile which has been surveyed to date. Comparing late Amratian Hierakonpolis and Naqada (where recent research is providing useful scientific information on settlements to complement Petrie's classic cemetery studies) to sites of the technologically similar Middle Mississippian culture of riverine eastern and midwestern North America (ca. 900-1540 A.D.), we would expect centralized chiefdoms in control of hundreds of miles of territory, able to field large armies and engage in long-distance trade. So far, the evidence for Amratian chiefdoms is inferential, resting on large richly furnished graves, maceheads, large scale proto-industrial pottery production, growing towns, dense populations and suggestions of growing conflict (models of fortified towns and arrows in big tombs). By the succeeding Gerzean period, there is no doubt that chiefdoms and, eventually, regional kingdoms emerged that directly foreshadowed Pharaonic civilization.

The Gerzean or Naqada II Period

The Gerzean Period evolved directly from the Amratian between about 3500 to 3400 B.C. Petrie once thought the Gerzean Period to be the result of an invasion by Southwest Asian peoples and Baumgartel felt it came about as a conquest of Upper Egypt by Delta people. We now know, however, that the Gerzean Period developed in the Upper Egyptian Nile Valley from indigenous roots and later spread southward into Nubia and northward into the western Delta.

There was a basic similarity and kinship between Predynastic Egyptian and Late Neolithic and A Group Nubian cultures in the fourth millennium B.C., evident especially in cemeteries like Kadada, 200 kilometers (120 miles) north of Khartoum in the Sudan. Thanks to recent discoveries at Kadada and Kadero, it is difficult to see the Nubian developments as due simply to diffusion or population movement from the North. Most probably we should speak of a southern or Nubian variant of the Predynastic, the development of which paralleled that of its northern neighbor until the beginning of the First Dynasty when the parallel Nubian culture was destroyed deliberately by the Pharaohs.

The Gerzean penetration of the Delta differed greatly from that of Nubia. Delta Neolithic culture was more diversified, reflecting the differing geography which encouraged the existence of more isolated centers along different branches of the river. So far, our best evidence for Gerzean settlement comes from the eastern Delta at sites like Minshat Abu Omar. Probably these places were oriented toward developing and protecting trade routes to Palestine and the Middle East. Abundant evidence for this trade exists in the form of wavy-handled Palestinian jars (fragments of which have been excavated as far south as Hierakonpolis), eastern artistic motifs, imported stone such as lapis lazuli and obsidian and improved metallurgical techniques. Throughout the Gerzean, people of the western and central Delta, the northernmost part of the Nile Valley just south of Cairo and the Fayum, retained their indigenous Lower Egyptian Neolithic way of life. Occasionally trade and possibly war occurred between the Delta inhabitants and their Southern neighbors. The eventual conquest of the central and western Delta peoples by later Protodynastic (Naqada III) kings, such as Narmer, was possibly motivated by a desire to dominate the flourishing Middle Eastern trade.

Our main evidence for Gerzean material culture and social and political organization comes from thousands of tombs excavated since Petrie's initial discoveries at Naqada in 1894-95. The black-topped Plum Red Ware characteristic of the preceding Amratian declined in popularity and the white cross-lined painted bowls totally disappeared. They were replaced by elaborately decorated jars sporting red painted designs on a buff or light-faced background. A key motif, which anticipated the familiar iconography and hieroglyphs of Dynastic times, was river boats, frequently propelled by oars and occasionally carrying cabins and shrines. Other familiar motifs include plants, animals, mountains, spirals, people and gods. Also evident on some of the pots usually carried on boats are totem-like standards on long poles which anticipate the later provincial or "Nome" standards and suggest the emergence of distinct territorial units. Other distinctive Gerzean pots are wavy-handled jars (both Palestinian imports and local copies) and "half-polished" Plum Red Ware bowls. Tombs were also stocked with large numbers of straw-tempered storage jars. The larger and more elaborate the tomb, the richer and more numerous were its contents. These included: pear-shaped maceheads; beautifully worked stone vases in a variety of shapes and made from attractive materials such as serpentine, marble, porphyry, amethyst, breccia, alabaster, schist and diorite; animal effigy slate palettes; fishtail "lanceheads"; finely made flint knives, which by the Late Gerzean are represented by incomparable ripple-flaked knives; cast copper tools and weapons; gold and silver jewelry and jar fittings; elaborate bone and ivory figurines and hair combs; and jewelry of imported semi-precious stones such as lapis lazuli and turquoise.

Gerzean tombs provide abundant evidence that the trend toward increasing social stratification noted in the late Amratian graves at Hierakonpolis had become a dominant theme in Predynastic culture. Big, elite structures are apparent everywhere and were usually set apart from lesser graves. Large, rectangular tombs, lined with mudbrick at Naqada and Hierakonpolis, suggest the presence of local kings. Tomb 100, the Painted Tomb at Hierakonpolis, measures about 5 meters (16 feet) by 2 meters (6.9 feet) by 1.5 meters (4.9 feet) deep and is elaborately decorated with wall paintings which recall the themes popular on the pottery of the time and which clearly anticipate the iconography of Dynastic times. In one scene, a local ruler raises his mace and prepares to dispatch several bound captives — a scene central to royal iconography for the next 3,500 years. Other scenes depict Southwest Asian motifs such as the "master of animals" — a man holding apart two rampant quadrupeds. Also shown are fighting soldiers with shields, herding, a procession of boats bearing shrines and a possible king. The scenes are organized in roughly horizontal "registers" or bands — anticipating one of the principal conventions used in classic Egyptian relief and paintings.

Beyond the existence of such early royal tombs, the sheer amount of wealth interred in many

Gerzean burials and the fine gradations of status reflected both in the size and elaboration of the tombs and in the grave goods themselves are striking. This was clearly a society on its way to statehood. The Painted Tomb shows kings, priests and warriors and contained a wide range of imported items, which imply the existence of merchants and traders. In addition to the pottery industry of Amratian times, new craft specialists, including metal, stone, ivory and bone workers, carpenters, weavers and painters, were plentiful.

Until recently, we had little knowledge of Gerzean settlements and architecture. Caton-Thompson's work at Hemamieh revealed what a small farming hamlet looked like with its simple circular huts, but the less controlled digs of Petrie at South Town Naqada (ancient Nubet), of Garstang at Mahasna and of Brunton in the Badari area produced more problematical results. Petrie did recover evidence of monumental architecture in the foundations of a 30 x 50 meter (100 x 165 foot) rectangular enclosure of mudbrick; the evidence hints at internally complex settlements paralleling the social complexity seen in Gerzean cemeteries. The inclusion of house models in Gerzean graves provides additional information on the superstructures of Gerzean buildings. A house model from el Amrah shows a rectangular house similar to contemporary village mudbrick structures, while a purchased piece of unknown provenance (Artifact 67) now at the Royal Ontario Museum and featured in "The First Egyptians," depicts an elaborate arched, ridge-pole house (probably the original was mud-plastered reeds) decorated with rows of animals resembling those on Gerzean pots. Finally, a small model interpreted as a town wall manned by two sentries was found at Abadiyeh and dates from the Amratian to Gerzean transition period.

Recent surveys and excavations in the desert at Hierakonpolis have supplemented our picture of the size and internal complexity of Gerzean sites. At one locality (HK-29A), the oldest known Egyptian temple complex focused around a parabolically or oval-shaped courtyard 14 meters (46 feet) wide and over 33 meters (108 feet) long and was discovered recently in the midst of a large settlement. The courtyard sloped uphill at a 9° angle and was paved with a succession of four or five smoothed clay floors, one of which contained footprints of animals and possibly of children. It was originally enclosed by a fence of mud-plastered reeds which was partially replaced at a later date by a more substantial mud brick wall. Flanking one wall was a long row of small rectangular buildings, perhaps storerooms, work spaces or residential areas. On the same side of the boundary wall was a gate flanked by two large wooden posts, the deep postholes of which have been uncovered. One end of the courtyard has still not been excavated.

On the opposite side of the courtyard across from the gate was the temple itself — a large building originally built on a wooden frame covered with mud-plastered wickerwork and mats. Four huge wooden columns perhaps 15 meters (49.2 feet) high formed the entrance to the temple which faced the courtyard. The remaining postholes for these columns are 1.7 meters (5.6 feet) deep. The temple interior was subdivided into a number of chambers by screen walls of mud-plastered reeds. The whole building resembles late Predynastic and Archaic representations of temples as well as the Dynastic model stone shrines built by King Djoser around his Step Pyramid (ca. 2700-2680 B.C.).

Only 200 meters (656 feet) from the Gerzean Temple complex at Hierakonpolis is a circular mound of small stones that Sir Guy Brunton first noted. Recent examination suggests a nucleated enclosure such as a fortified palace compound that had numerous rooms radiating out from a central open court. Parallels are known from Protodynastic sites in the Sinai. Both the temple enclosure and possible palace are only 2 kilometers (1.2 miles) from the Painted Tomb. The close interrelationship between palace, temple and royal necropolis which apparently began in the mid-Gerzean remained characteristic of great administrative centers throughout Egyptian history.

By the end of the Gerzean, trends toward political unification and competition between regional states had reached a critical point, as indicated by a protective wall enclosure unearthed at Hierakonpolis. This three meter (10 foot) thick wall was built during the transition of Gerzean to Protodynastic times.

The Protodynastic or Naqada III Period

The Protodynastic evolved directly from the late Gerzean, continuing earlier trends toward political and economic centralization. The century or so before Narmer and Aha (ca. 3200-3100 B.C.) was a time of ferment as powerful regional kings contended for dominance of the Nile Valley. In attempting to extend the Dynastic chronology back in time, many Egyptologists have tried to reconstruct a sequence of Protodynastic rulers based on cryptic references to semi-mythological monarchs who ruled before Menes, found in early king lists (e.g. The Palermo Stone, ca. 2400 B.C.). Some concrete evidence for such kings is provided by the Scorpion Macehead and by several tombs at Abydos which Petrie attributed to rulers, such as "Ka" and "Ro"

(Irj-Hor), who preceded Narmer. Petrie assigned these kings to his "Dynasty 0." More recently, German Egyptologists like Kaiser and Dreyer have tried to redo and improve his sequence. Another term proposed by Petrie, the "Semainean," roughly corresponds to the Protodynastic (Naqada III) Period but has dropped out of favor because it is archaeologically impossible to separate some of its material from finds of proven First Dynasty dates.

Archaeologically, the replacement of the old Plum Red Ware with a "Hard Orange" ware tempered with ground shell or bone (see Adams' essay) characterizes the Protodynastic. Red paint remained a popular decorative medium, but abstract motifs such as dots, commas and parallel wavy lines (possible water signs) replaced the realistic representations of the Gerzean Period. Throughout the Protodynastic, wavy handles became smaller and more stylized until they were replaced with a single row of string impressions shown on First Dynasty cylindrical jars. One of the most characteristic mortuary forms was a cylindrical jar painted with imitation nets. Black tops — a key criterion of Predynastic pottery — became very rare and were confined to small jars.

Other characteristically Protodynastic artifacts include: ripple-flaked flint knives with ivory and gold handles decorated with scenes of battles, animal processions and goddesses; animal effigy flints; intricately carved ivory handles, plaques and inlay; well-made wooden furniture with carved bull's legs; large ceremonial slate palettes (like the Narmer Palette) that show scenes of hunts, warfare and processions of animals carved in shallow relief; ceremonial carved maceheads (like the giant Scorpion Macehead); beautifully made stone bowls and jars — the latter occasionally decorated with gold foil; carved lapis lazuli jewelry and figurines; the increased use of foreign imports like obsidian, turquoise and lapis; signs of continuing Middle Eastern influence in artistic motifs; more widespread use of cast copper tools and weapons; and the beginning of recognizable hieroglyphic script.

The tombs and cemeteries of the Protodynastic reflect the emergence of large states in the Nile Valley. The elite precincts of late Amratian and Gerzean cemeteries evolved into true royal necropoleis at sites like Hierakonpolis and Qustul, preceding the great mortuary complexes of Archaic and Old Kingdom times.

In addition to distinctions of wealth and power, tomb types of the period suggest the presence of two distinct cultural provinces which may correspond to the ancient distinction between Upper and Lower Egypt. In northern, central and part of southern Egypt (from the eastern Delta to Hierakonpolis) elite tombs consisted of rectangular, brick-lined pits, while poorer graves were generally subrectangular to rectangular and unlined. From southern Egypt into Nubia (from Hierakonpolis and el Kab to Qustul) another style of tomb design was used for both rich and poor burials. This southern style consisted of an oval or long rectangular pit with a separate burial chamber set at roughly right angles to the main pit and divided from it by one or more large stone slabs.

Recent discoveries at site HK-6 at Hierakonpolis, a Protodynastic royal cemetery located along a dry desert stream or "wadi," suggest that the "northern" and "southern" style elite tombs were positioned symbolically, with the southern variant at the upstream or "Upper Egyptian" end of the site and the northern variant at the downstream or "Lower Egyptian" end. The fact that the southern style tomb is rock cut — the earliest in Egypt — emphasizes its extreme importance as does the presence of an animal cemetery around it. Given the popularity of animals and animal processions in the royal iconography of the time, the presence of an animal precinct around the stone tomb reinforces its royal associations and perhaps indicates the different gods or provinces which supported the king. So far, animal remains identified include: cattle, crocodile, elephant, gazelle, dog and baboon. There is preliminary evidence of crude mummification as well as deliberate placement of certain species to correspond with their symbolic divine attributes. For example the baboons, associated with the dawn, are located on the eastern periphery of the cemetery.

The Royal Protodynastic cemetery at Hierakonpolis is further linked to later royal mortuary complexes by the discovery that wooden mortuary temples modeled after the shrines of the period once covered the large brick-lined tombs.

Regrettably, little is known about the settlements of the period. Only from Nekhen (Kom el Ahmar or ancient Hierakonpolis) do we have any architectural evidence and that comes from a limited stratigraphic exposure. Nevertheless, what we do have suggests that domestic and religious buildings employed the older techniques of wood and mud-plastered reed, although many of the larger structures of the period used mud brick and roughly shaped stone. The large mud brick enclosure wall begun in slightly earlier times at Nekhen persisted until the end of the Protodynastic and was then

Double sieving at Hierakonpolis.

succeeded by a series of well-made mud brick rooms which apparently belonged to a First Dynasty administrative or industrial complex. The earlier discoveries of Quibell and Green revealed a large rough stone revetment filled with clean sand. This structure was probably of Protodynastic age and would have supported a large wood and mud-plastered reed temple.

By analyzing the overall Protodynastic settlement pattern in the Hierakonpolis region at this time (an area that was almost certainly the capital of Upper Egypt) we note a marked trend toward concentrating the population around the administrative center of Nekhen. The fact that this trend was maintained in the face of a local rainy period which would have opened up the desert for possible settlement emphasizes both the strength of the government and its stake in keeping population in a small, easily defended and readily mobilized area. The military importance of towns and cities during the Protodynastic Period is emphasized repeatedly by the artistic representations of walled and bastioned settlements shown on the great ceremonial palettes and also suggested by the hieroglyph ⊗ for town —

a circle (town wall) with a cross (two intersecting streets?) inside it.

Postscript - The Archaic Period

Around 3100 B.C., Egypt was united under the first king of the First Dynasty. According to Egyptian legend and the ancient king lists, his name was "Menes." According to most modern Egyptologists Menes should probably be identified with Aha (or Hor-Aha), a successor of Narmer. Others give the credit to Narmer. In either case, the material culture and subsistence economy of Archaic Egypt under the first two dynasties (ca. 3100-2700 B.C.) derived directly from Predynastic antecedents. The big differences we see reflect the extreme centralization of power under a Pharaonic bureaucracy and the diversion of increasingly large amounts of surplus goods to the royal mortuary cult. Only gradually did Egypt assume a more homogenized look as the king fixed boundaries, monopolized trade and expanded the royal workshops to more thoroughly control the production of desirable mortuary goods. These goods allowed the king to reward loyal clients and furnish his own vastly expanded tomb and mortuary temple. Some of the most striking technological developments of this period, such as in copper metallurgy and stone vase manufacture, directly reflect the demands of the mortuary cult and the use of royal patronage.

Although the Archaic Period is technically historical in that we do have written names of kings, the few inscriptions are very short and often difficult to read. Therefore, our dating and broader cultural knowledge of this epoch is still heavily dependent on the techniques of archaeology. One of the main questions which has concerned Egyptologists working with the Archaic Period is the true location of the royal tombs. Most agree that they were at Abydos, but a case can still be made, despite recent arguments, that the great tombs unearthed by Walter Emery at Saqqara were royal cenotaphs or "symbolic" tombs.

Another question of Egyptological concern involves the end of the Archaic and its last king (Khasekhem/Khasekhemui). During the Second Dynasty (ca. 2900-2700 B.C.) it appears that there was a civil war or at least a partial collapse of royal authority. The last two kings of the Dynasty, Peribsen and Khasekhemui, were the only ones buried at the ancestral cemetery of Abydos and the only ones to take the unprecedented step of writing their names below the stylized Set animal as well as the traditional hawk of Horus. Once royal authority was reasserted, the stage was set for the classic period of Egyptian history — The Old Kingdom (ca. 2700-2230 B.C.). With the passing of Khasekhemui, Abydos was abandoned as a royal cemetery and soon great pyramid complexes were being raised at Saqqara just outside the capital city of Memphis, near modern Cairo. The beginning of the Pyramid Age — the zenith of Pharaonic power — followed as Egypt evolved beyond the organizational structures and forms of its Predynastic and Archaic years.

As a final comment on the unprecedented political centralization reached under the Old Kingdom, we must note that the rise of the Egyptian state was achieved at the expense of the Pharaohs' ordinary subjects. Their tombs during the fabled Pyramid Age were but impoverished hovels compared to those of their Predynastic ancestors.

Sorting potsherds with Fort Khasekhemui in the distance.

Pots and potsherds are the most abundant and durable cultural remains of antiquity preserved in Egypt. At a large necropolis such as that at Saqqara near Cairo, a sea of pottery sherds on the desert surface represents the debris of four thousand years of human activity. Pottery is breakable but durable, normally has a limited useful life, is produced relatively easily and is subject to prevailing fashion. Therefore, pottery can be analyzed as a tool in relative dating — a technique for determining that object "x" is older than object "y." In the Egyptian historic period, inscriptions and the associated pottery often occur in contexts that can be dated and linked; in this way a framework of date ranges for the pottery types can be produced. Pottery analysis is most relevant for the Predynastic Period, which had no written language.

I. Description and Analysis of Pottery Types and Sequence Dating

Introduction

The British excavator William Matthew Flinders Petrie worked at the end of the nineteenth century and was a pioneer in the field of archaeological ceramics both from Egypt and Palestine. He was the first Egyptologist and, like the English pioneer archaeologist General Pitt-Rivers, he learned to "read the pottery" from the sites.

In the 1890s, at the time of Flinders Petrie's initial work on the Predynastic assemblages from cemeteries, no stratified village sites had been excavated with the goal of recognizing sequences of levels which could be correlated by means of potsherds to give an archaeological progression. Petrie first iden-

25. Roll Rim Jar; Middle Gerzean; The Petrie Museum, University College London (UC 6340).

PREDYNASTIC POTTERY

by Barbara Adams
Curator, Petrie Museum of Egyptian Archaeology,
University College London

tified the distinctive pottery types and then devised a system of relative dating or seriation (which he termed Sequence Dating), based on the increase and decrease in the styles and frequencies of pottery types and other objects in the graves. Thus Petrie established a chronological and typological framework for the Upper Egyptian Predynastic cultures that is still the basis for work today.

Types

Petrie identified several types of hand-made pottery. The black-topped red group, or B-class, comprises vessels made of black- to red-firing Nile silt. The vessels have a polished red surface and a blackened area below the rim that probably was produced by placing the vessel upside down in reducing organic material during or immediately after firing. The polished red vessels, or P-class, are closely allied and have the same surface treatment but lack the blackened rims and interiors. An all-black polished ware (in Petrie's F for fancy class) has the same fabric and surface treatment as the polished red pottery. Petrie's strangely named white cross-lined, or C-class, is polished red pottery with the addition of a light painted decoration in calcareous clay. The fabric of all these fine Nile silt wares contains very fine micaceous sand, but whether this was an added temper or a constituent of the alluvial clay is not certain. The use of temper apparently varied regionally. Animal dung, which contains fine chaff, was added to give body. Whether a slip was applied to the surface of the pots is not always easy to determine in hand specimens, because the pots were polished with a pebble at the leather-hard stage before firing. Most pots seemingly were coated with red ocher (iron oxide). Patterns of the burnishing usually were placed horizontally around the rim and vertically on the body of the pots.

Petrie described another Nile silt fabric, rough or R-class, that is a coarse pottery, fired light brown to orange and often straw-tempered. Proven to be settlement utilitarian ware, it did not generally appear in quantity in the graves until the second phase of the Predynastic sequence (Naqada II). Apparently in the earlier phase only the "best" tableware was deemed good enough for the dead; later, quantity was equally important. These pots have no surface treatment, apart from smoothing and the occasional incised design or relief, although some may have been self-slipped. The shapes are shared with other categories, particularly the P- and L-classes. The last Nile silt group that Petrie described includes the Nubian pottery (N-class), which was made from a less homogeneous clay, usually was fired grey to brown, and was imported into Egypt starting in Naqada II time. This pottery often has incised or impressed geometric designs, sometimes filled with white.

A fine calcareous clay (marl) from the soft shale in the desert wadis was used to manufacture the D-, W-, and L-classes, which fired orange to pink at lower temperatures and buff or greenish cream at higher temperatures (see analysis section). The surfaces were smoothed or sometimes slipped. The decorated (D-class) had designs in an ocher wash of plum-red hue. Petrie defined another group as W-class or "wavy-handled," which today is considered a misnomer because, strictly speaking, its definition has nothing to do with the fabric or overall surface treatment but refers to the form of the pottery which had two applied wavy handles in relief. The presumed sequential change in the wavy-handled types, shown in Figure 4, was the basis of Petrie's Sequence Dating.

Petrie's Late (L-class) is an unacceptable grouping of pottery that includes various fabrics and surface treatments (straw-tempered wares, marl wares, red-slipped and washed wares, slipped and streak-burnished wares, etc.) linked together by their chronological position at the end of the Predynastic sequence. Many of the L-class types overlap with those later grouped by Petrie in his corpus of Protodynastic pottery, which actually covers the latest Predynastic to Protodynastic pottery, now generally called Naqada III, as well as some of the Early Dynastic types.

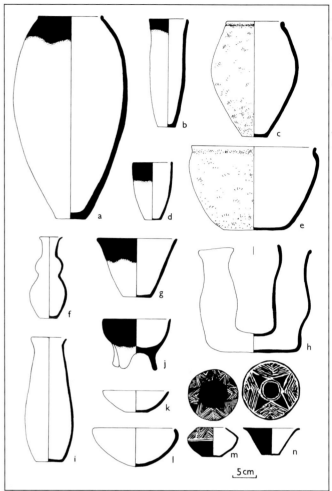

FIGURE 1. A selection of the corpus shapes of Naqada I (Amratian) pottery (after Petrie). a, b, d, g, j: black-topped red (Petrie's B-class); c, e: straw tempered (Petrie's R-class); f, h, i, k, l: polished red (Petrie's P-class); m, n: white cross-lined (Petrie's C-class).

The selected typical pottery corpuses here (Figures 1, 2, 3 and 4) are grouped in the major divisions of the Predynastic sequence that Petrie established. Within the classes, Petrie further divided the pottery by form from the most open types, such as bowls, to the most closed, such as bottles. The first group (Figure 1) illustrates some of the pottery types typical of the Amratian, or Naqada I, Period and includes the black-topped red, polished red, white cross-lined and rough Nile silt wares such as dishes, bowls, jars and bottles. The next group (Figure 2) covers the Gerzean, or Naqada II, Period and shows the continuation of the black-topped and polished red vessels with changes in shape, the expansion of the R (straw-tempered) types, and the introduction of the black polished Nile silt ware and the plum-painted calcareous ware, as well as the plain types. The next corpus extract (Figure 3) illustrates Petrie's version of the evolution of wavy-handled pottery types, from the earliest squat rounded jars with exaggerated handles (thought to copy Palestinian

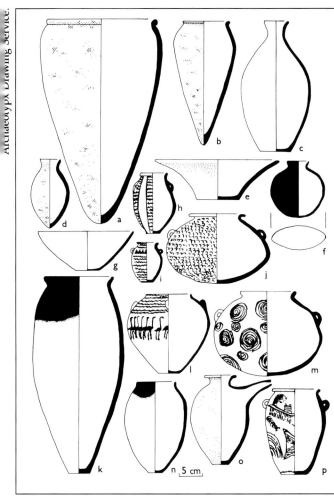

FIGURE 2. A selection of corpus shapes of Naqada II (Gerzean) pottery (after Petrie). a, b, d, e: straw tempered (Petrie's R-class); c, g: polished red (Petrie's P-class); f: black polished (Petrie's F-class); h, i, j, l, m, n, p: plum red painted buff/pink marl (Petrie's D-class); k, n: black-topped red (Petrie's B-class); o: smooth buff/pink marl (Petrie's L-class).

prototypes, Figure 3a,b), through the tapering Egyptian versions (Figure 3c-g) to the last phase of Predynastic vessels (Figure 3h-j) and the Protodynastic to Early Dynastic cylinder vases (Figure 3k,l) with only vestigial wavy lines for handles. The last selected assemblage (Figure 4) illustrates Protodynastic, or Naqada III, pottery and covers the continuation of the P- and R-classes, the marl wares with simplified decoration of this phase and the introduction of the L-class. The black-topped red vessels no longer appear.

For ease of comprehension, the fabric of the figured pottery types is also illustrated. The polished red surface is shown as plain; the black-topped red as black on plain; the white cross-lined on red polished as white on black; the R, or straw-tempered, ware as stippled; and the L-, D- and W-classes (marl wares) as more lightly stippled to distinguish them from the Nile silt types. In 1945, the Canadian Walter Federn proposed a revision of Petrie's classes that

Winifred Needler later espoused. Federn retained Petrie's B-, P-, C-, R-, N-, and W-classes but added two new classes: B1 covers bowls that are polished black on the interior and red outside; B-P covers the black polished wares in Petrie's Fancy group and thereby eliminates the F-class. Federn then broke down the unsatisfactory Late class into three classes. S (for smooth) covers the calcareous plain pottery, usually large storage vessels. P1 covers a polished red surface treatment on S (= marl fabric). P2 covers half-polished bowls of similar fabric with a red slip or wash over the interior and just below the rim on the exterior. Type P2 is indicated in Figure 4a with a broken line shading below the rim. In seriations of whole pots from graves and in quantified sherds from the settlement beneath the city at Hierakonpolis, type P2 has proved to be a chronological marker for the Naqada II and the transition between Naqada II and III.

Seriation

Various refinements have been made to Petrie's seriation method as well as to his divisions of pottery types. Petrie achieved his seriation method in 1901, without benefit of modern technology, after shuffling and sorting slips marked with the pottery types for nine hundred graves selected from the four thousand excavated at Hu, Abadiyeh (Diospolis Parva), Naqada and Ballas. Petrie then assigned stages to cover the inception, flourishing and degradation of pottery types so that, after leaving a space for earlier material, the Predynastic had a range of Sequence Date 30 to Sequence Date 39 for the Amratian (Naqada I), S.D.40-52 for the Gerzean (Naqada II), and S.D.54-79 for what Petrie called the Semainean (Naqada III). His later work at Abydos and Tarkhan took the Sequence Dates 77-84 into the First and Second Dynasties. All other categories of objects were fitted into the Sequence Dating framework, which is intended to indicate the order of development and the relation of objects to each other and not to be a measure of absolute time. Therefore, the Sequence Date numbers do not necessarily have the same values.

While Petrie's achievement remains innovative and classic, the most accepted refinement in recent years has been that of Werner Kaiser, a German, who seriated the pottery from a cemetery excavated by Oliver Myers at Armant and produced a sequence of further sub-divisions: Naqada I (= S.D.30 38), Naqada II a,b (= S.D.38/40-45), Naqada II c,d (= S.D.40/45-63) and Naqada III (= S.D.63-80). He also showed that Petrie's reliance on wavy-handled pottery for Sequence Dating was unsound, so that S.D.40-80 are dubious. There is still some controversy about which king is to be accepted as the first of a united Egypt, so that the beginning date of the First Dynasty can fluctuate between S.D.77-80. Naqada III and Dynasty I types obviously overlap somewhat, but overall Kaiser's refined divisions of the Upper Egyptian Predynastic cultural sequence have gained wide acceptance. Further confirmation was produced in a computerized seriation of the pottery from a cemetery at El Amrah by Barry Kemp in 1982. Kemp defined the three major temporal groups, suggested a break between Naqada I and II later than Petrie set, and suggested a subdivision within group II. None of Kemp's refinements clash with the scheme of stages, or Stufen, worked out by Kaiser.

Getrude Caton-Thompson was another pioneer who brought the era of sherd studies into Egyptian archaeology when she excavated the stratified village settlement of Hemamieh in Middle Egypt in the 1920s, confirming the phases of the Predynastic set up by Petrie. She and Guy Brunton also identified another cultural assemblage from the settlement and a cemetery at Badari which they termed the Badarian. The pottery of this group is similar to that of the Neolithic cultures of Lower Nubia and to the succeeding Amratian. The black-topped Nile silt vessels with a characteristic ripple burnish over the brown surface are among the finest pottery ever produced in the Nile Valley (Artifact 1). Other artifacts are prototypes of those which continued into Naqada I & II. The Badarian was found beneath the Amratian and Gerzean levels at Hemamieh, proving that Petrie had also been correct in allowing a space for cultures to precede S.D.30.

Hierakonpolis System

Modern analyses of pottery from the settlement sites of Hierakonpolis now being excavated require that whole assemblages be studied and defined. The contents of one tomb or a limited cemetery area do not provide convenient boundaries for these modern analyses. In Hierakonpolis, the quantity of the Predynastic pottery sherds scattered over the desert is simply staggering and produces a sense of wonder at the production of this indestructable material by early Egyptian potters. A system of sherd analysis developed at Hierakonpolis has fabric or ware divisions similar to the groups described above, but further subdivided: I = Straw-tempered (R); II = Plum Red (B, P, N); III = Grit-tempered (R); IV = Straw and Stone-tempered (R); V = Crushed calcium carbonate (L, W, D); VI = Undetermined; VII = Sherd temper; VIII = Marl (L, W, D); IX = Sand (L); X = Marl/Crushed Calcium Carbonate (L, W, D); XI = Dung (R, N); XII = Marl/Nile silt (L, W, D); XIII = Marl/Straw (L); XXX = Palestinian; and so on. Then the pottery is further subdivided according to the part of the vessel from which it comes, for instance rim, body or base, and the general shape classes are defined (dishes, bowls, large and small storage jars, vases, bottles). Rims and bases are then used to build up a shape typology, and details of surface treatment, such as incision, painting, slipping or burnishing, are added. Every type of sherd is included in the quantification; the observations are then coded and large numbers (over 350,000 sherds from one part of a single Predynastic settlement!) can be recorded for analysis. Because of the large numbers involved, computers are used as an aid to analysis. The results obtained are correlated with the excavated archaeological units and strata. The results, which can give an indication of functional areas and pottery evolution, are based on the frequency of certain pottery types. The earlier corpuses were set up from the whole pots, mostly derived from tombs. The ceramicist on a modern excavation needs a knowledge of the established fabric and corpus types and the revised systems; an ability to identify, sort, quantify, code and record the thousands of sherds that a day's digging can produce from even a modest excavation quandrant of 10 meters; the application to spot the potential joins in sherds from closed units such as graves; and the ability to work with other experts, such as geochemists, to sharpen the precision of field analysis.

Manufacture and Analysis of Pottery

After the wet clay was kneaded to a uniform consistency, and any temper was added to reduce its stickiness and assist drying, the pots were shaped. During the Predynastic the smaller vessels were hand-formed from lumps of clay, and the larger vessels were coil made. In the later Predynastic and Protodynastic the bodies of the pots were handmade, and the rims show the manufacturing marks of hand-turning, achieved by rotating the pot on a tournette or stand. The potter's wheel was not in use in Egypt until the Old Kingdom. The pots were air dried, burnished if necessary to ensure impermeability, and then baked. Ancient kiln sites are still fairly uncommon in Egypt, although depictions of them are known from historic tomb scenes; but the remains of quite a number of Predynastic kilns have been discovered in the desert sites at Hierakonpolis.

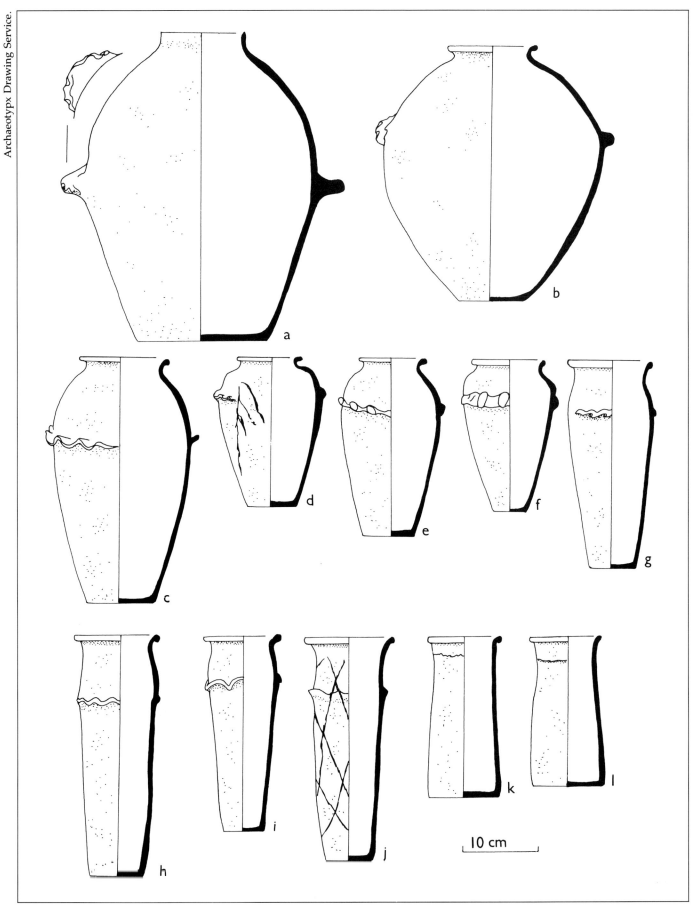

FIGURE 3. The evolution of the wavy handled pottery types as envisaged by Petrie from the full bodied jars (a and b) which copied Palestinian shapes, through the typical Gerzean shapes (c, d, e, f, g), to the Protodynastic (h, i, j) and Early Dynastic (k, l) cylinders with vestigial wavy lines.

One such kiln site for straw-tempered pottery was excavated in the Great Wadi. This kiln is an updraft type with a ring wall of fire dogs or mud-brick andirons shaped like dog biscuits that are placed vertically to support large vessels containing smaller pots. Acacia wood and Tamarisk wood, from trees in the wadi, were used to fire the kiln; dung was probably also used. Another kiln in a late Amratian settlement was a simpler affair consisting of shallow basins supporting large storage jars that functioned as "saggers"—containers for holding pots to be fired. The oval kiln was surrounded by a low ring wall of mud; fuel (probably dung) was heaped over the saggers, weighted down with old sherds and ignited. Other kilns, where the fine polished red and black-topped red pottery of Naqada I and II were produced for deposit in the wadi cemetery, used natural wind currents and are currently under investigation.

Various modern analytical techniques are available for the study of pottery. Thermoluminescence (TL) is the emission of photons of visible light from electrons recombining with atoms when material is heated. TL begins to accumulate when pottery is fired above 500°C and it can be measured on re-firing to estimate the length of time that has elapsed between firings. This technique has been used to confirm that some suspect painted pots are Naqada II in date but were painted and re-fired in modern times. It has also been used to date sherds from the stratified site of Hemamieh. The date ranges given suggest that not only did the Badarian have a long time span from perhaps as early as 5500 B.C., it also seems to have continued and overlapped with the Amratian, or until 3800 B.C. Generally, this technique is not completely reliable for precise dating.

X-ray fluorescence and neutron activation analysis can be used to identify in great detail the elements present in an artifact. This information can help geologists and geochemists identify the sediment source. These techniques have important implications for the local manufacture, production centers, foreign imports and trading patterns of pottery.

The constituents of pottery can also be analyzed by petrography, a geological method used for the identification of minerals in rocks. A small section of a pottery sherd is ground very thin and then examined under a polarizing microscope to identify the larger mineral grains in the pottery. Mineralogical changes can also indicate the firing temperature of the pottery because some minerals alter form at temperatures above 500°C. This type of study is useful in the identification of foreign pottery

5. Vase; Amratian; (c) The Detroit Institute of Arts, Founders Society Purchase, Acquisitions Fund (79.44.1)

imported into Egypt as well as of early Egyptian pottery found outside the Nile Valley. Reasonably homogeneous Nile clay was the principal raw material used in Egypt and it is recognized in thin sections by the presence of quartz grains, mica flakes, feldspars and heavy minerals. Chopped straw, used by early Egyptians as a temper, left impressions that commonly are recognizable. Egyptian marl wares are defined by a calcareous matrix with a temper of calcite and quartz, and occasional silt-sized grains of quartz and mica; heavy mineral grains indicate that Nile clay was sometimes mixed with the marl. Radiogeochemical analysis by neutron activation has now revealed that the equivalent of marl ware at Hierakonpolis, which fired a hard orange to pink, resulted from the addition of crushed calcium carbonate (bone, shell, stone) to Nile silt. The firing temperatures of the Nile siltwares were in the range of 700°C-800°C, and the harder marl wares were fired between about 750° and 850°C. Re-firing experiments on red polished ware and rough, straw-tempered sherds have confirmed a probable firing temperature of 700°C-800°C. In contrast, Canaanite pottery, the chief foreign group traded into Egypt in the Predynastic and Early Dynastic periods, was made from shale and marl, often rich in microfossils, tempered with crushed carbonate rock (limestone, calcite and dolomite), and fired below 750°C. On an excavation such as Hierakonpolis it is possible, with experience, to identify the "foreigners" among the sherds even in small pieces of small specimens, so different is their fabric and temper from the Egyptian wares.

II. Interpretation of Pottery Decoration, Shapes and Use in Trade

The discovery of Predynastic cultures at the end of the last century has led to numerous and speculative interpretations of the religious beliefs and practices of the period. Inference has to be based on the funerary customs, depictions found on the objects, and some of the objects themselves, such as figurines. The true picture of religious belief in the Predynastic may include quite a few of the suggestions which have been made, but one or two basic beliefs are certain. First, later religious and funerary practices clearly show that the Egyptians believed in an after-life and made provision for it in their burials. The practice of elaborate burial of the dead together with grave goods indicates that this belief goes back to the Predynastic and continued to develop in Dynastic times. The Egyptians also took various precautions to safeguard the souls of their deceased through prophylactic amulets, spells and rituals. Of course, this custom is known from other ancient and modern societies. Amulets certainly existed in the Predynastic; that there were ceremonies can be inferred from rare depictions.

Secondly, in later times there was a pantheon of numerous gods and goddesses, many of whom were linked to, or personified by, animals. From the earliest times the Egyptians observed a predetermined pattern in the natural world. This pattern implied superhuman powers, and a basic order gave their religion a long tradition of conservatism. The depictions of various animals in the Predynastic sometimes are interpreted as representations of deities, or as prophylactic devices to ward off evil or to ensure good hunting. Some figures were no doubt connected with ensuring fecundity, given a probable high infant mortality rate and the need to encourage the continued gift of the Nile's fertility. One of the most attractive ideas to re-emerge recently is that the motifs on the decorated pottery and the potmarks are closely related to the development of the hieroglyphic script, which existed from the Early Dynastic period, and that they convey messages. Precisely what these messages actually say is still not agreed upon; however, a multi-entry dictionary could be compiled from the various suggestions made since 1896. The depictions found on Predynastic pottery are therefore worthy of study as an adjunct to the chronological and technical aspects of analysis, and the following is a summary of the interpretations of the decorative devices.

The design elements on white cross-lined (C-class) Naqada I pottery are restricted to geometric devices, plants, domestic and desert animals (Figure 5b), hippopotami (Figure 5a) and reptiles. Depictions of humans (Figure 5c) and boats (Figure 5d) are rarer. The geometric shapes found on the interior of bowls and platters may be reminiscent of later hieroglyphic signs that express geographic terms in historic Egypt, such as those for province ⊞⊞⊞ (SPZT) and town ⊗ (NIWT). The hieroglyph for land and horizon is an oval ⬭, which is not only a motif featured on some of the bowls but is also the shape of some of the early Predynastic dishes. Thus, what seems to be a simple geometric device of stacked triangles or chevrons, sometimes interspersed with plant designs, around an oval or circle (Figure 1n), may represent a territorial statement about a flat region or country within surrounding mountain ranges, a description of Egypt itself.

The hippopotamus was certainly respected and perhaps even worshipped. Apart from the depictions of them painted around the interior of bowls (Figure 5a and Artifact 9), amulets of pottery, bone and ivory in this form were also popular in the Amratian. From the prolific use of hippopotamus ivory in Predynastic and Dynastic times, it is certain that the animal was hunted. Perhaps the charming early depictions served as protective devices against the animal's marauding habits later to be identified with Seth, the god of chaotic forces.

Human figures occasionally appear on C-class pots. The man and woman in Figure 5d are said to be dancing; they have also been identified as the great cow-goddess and her male consort. A cow-goddess is known from a relief of a cow's head, with five stars on the horns, on a slate palette from a grave at Gerzeh and from various potmarks; she is more likely to be Bat, the cow-goddess of Upper Egypt, than Hathor, the cow-goddess of the Nile and fertility. The interior of a dish (Figure 5b) has been identified as the top view of a boat with the oars on each side, but this unique piece is unprovenanced and its authenticity is unknown.

When we consider the depictions on Gerzean pottery, the repertoire is greater and consequently open to differing interpretations. Certain elements or combinations of elements seem to be standard, such as sycamore trees; shields; ostriches; gazelles; water

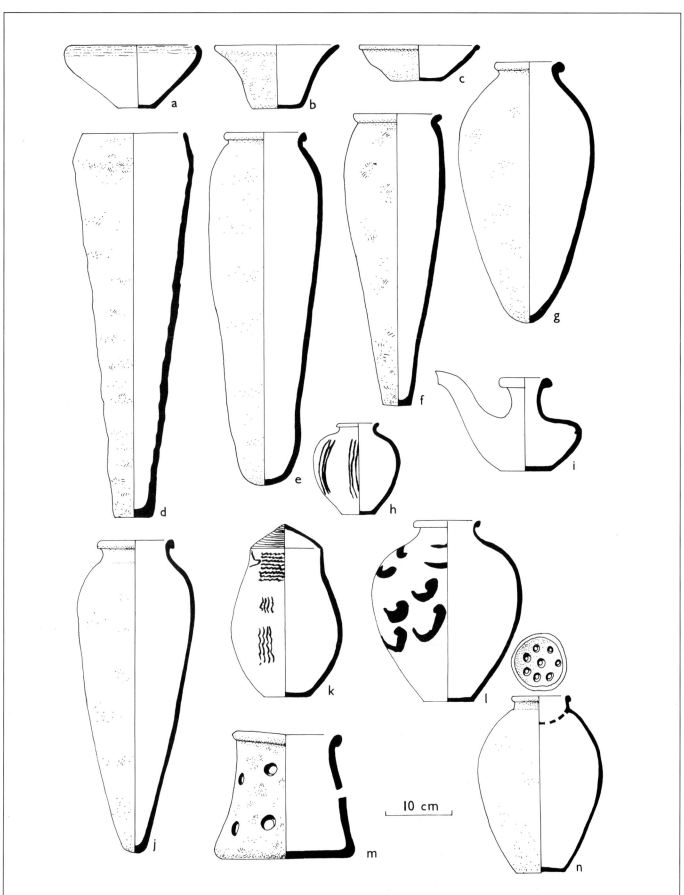

Archaeotypx Drawing Service.

10 cm

FIGURE 4. A selection of corpus shapes of Naqada III (Protodynastic) pottery (after Petrie). a: buff/pink marl ware bowl with red slipped interior and exterior rim; b, d, f, m: straw tempered (Petrie's R-class); e, g, j: buff/pink marl (Petrie's L-class); i: polished red (Petrie's P-class); h, k, l: buff/pink painted marl ware (Petrie's D-class); n: marl ware jar with integral strainer in mouth (Petrie's L-class).

lines; SSS signs; boats with cabins, standards, banners and oars; the Naqada plants; and spirals and hills (Figure 5e-g and Artifact 25). Some authors do not accept all the depictions listed above. The identification of the boats may represent watered land with the residence of a chief, rather than a cabin shrine. The Naqada plant, which seems to sprout from a small pot, has been variously identified as an aloe, a sycamore tree, a rush with shoots or a relative of the date palm. The smaller divided tree is usually accepted as a sycamore, a sacred tree in historical depictions from which the goddess Hathor poured libations. The third motif which appears beneath the boats in some scenes (Figure 5f) has been suggested as a cow's skin stretched out on a pole to dry, and a similar determinative 𓏏 appears in the hieroglyphic word for shield. The identification of the long-necked birds, which usually appear in rows (Figure 2l), has varied between ostrich and flamingo. Although nobody disputes that the wavy lines at the top and bottom of the scenes denote water (Figure 2h-j; Figure 5e,g), the scattered SSS signs (Figure 5e,f) have been called numbers, libation water or notations of weight. The spirals which sometimes appear on pots alone (Figure 2m and Artifact 28) have been interpreted as nummulitic limestone, bread, a sign meaning "surround everything" and as a simple decorative motif. Fortunately, the blocked triangles which are usually linked together (Figure 2i) are universally identified as depictions of hills. These decorated pots are rare in settlement sites and not as frequent in graves as other types of pottery, and it is probable that they were meant to confer special benefits on the dead. Perhaps the often repeated motifs were simply meant to ensure a continuation of spiritual life in an abundant Nilotic environment; or in a more sophisticated way, they may be spells recording life, death and guaranteed resurrection.

Some of these pots (Figure 5g) include schematic human figures. The goddess with raised arms is usually the central figure, with smaller male attendants. An ithyphalic male figure is found occasionally, depicted wearing a double-plumed head-dress, and was later the iconography of the fertility god Min of Koptos. Many of the design elements on the decorated pottery are repeated in incised drawings on the rocks of the wadis adjacent to the Nile valley from Upper Egypt to Nubia and in the late Gerzean Painted Tomb at Hierakonpolis.

The standards on poles which appear on the boats (Figure 5e and Artifact 25) are generally accepted as divine emblems and perhaps also as the ensigns of clans or nomes. There is some agreement here because some of the standards, such as the crossed arrows of the goddess Neith 𓋃 and the emblem of the god Min 𓏠, are virtually identical with those of historic times, while other signs are otherwise identifiable. There is also an early tradition of incised marks, some of which represent animals, plants, boats and inferred signs similar to those on the painted pots, while others may be the owner's marks or descriptions of the contents or locality. These graffiti are found on sherds from settlements as well as on pots in graves, and can justifiably be seen as a stage in the development of writing in which individual signs already had symbolic meanings, later to be followed by the phonetic values of the hieroglyphic script. Although contact with Mesopotamia may have provided some impetus, the early sherds provide evidence that the hieroglyphic script evolved indigenously in Egypt.

Interrelationships

Undoubtedly the earliest pottery was made in imitation of gourds and baskets. The shapes and incised decoration of Neolithic pottery were inspired by their hemispherical and plaited structures, devices that were retained in the Nubian tradition. This type of interrelationship continued throughout the Predynastic as the designs of vessels in pottery and stone were mutually echoed, so that the whole cultural assemblage had a unity. Stone vase shapes copied pottery shapes and *vice versa*, so that poor man's versions of vessels in hard stones were available. For instance, difficult-to-work stones, such as basalt and breccia, were copied in black pottery (Figure 2f), or their structures were imitated with paint (Figure 3j). The Protodynastic cylinder vases of calcite were also made in pottery (Figure 3k,l), from which their vestigial wavy-line decoration was derived. A class of theriomorphic (animal-shaped) vessels in stone or pottery, inspired by mammals, birds, fish and reptiles, arose in the Badarian. The hippopotamus was a chief feature of the Amratian, but the most popular zoomorphic pottery vessels in the Gerzean depicted birds (Artifact 10) and fish (Artifact 35). It seems the animal-shaped vessels, like the decorated pottery, were meant to confer upon the deceased an after-life abundant in Nile fauna. Pottery model boats, which copied papyrus river skiffs, can be included in the same genre, and the symbolism conveyed by the funeral boat in historic times was the journey through the underworld.

Native Nubian ware (N-class above) is readily distinguishable from Egyptian pottery and has been found spasmodically in graves and settlement sites in Egypt dating to early Naqada II, by which time the Gerzean culture had probably spread into Lower Nubia. But not until Naqada III to Dynasty I times did the frequency of Nubian pottery (A-Group) increase in southern Upper Egypt, while Egyptian influence reached as far as the second cataract of the Nile below Aswan. The cemeteries of the Nubian A-Group excavated in Lower Nubia contain graves that include typical Egyptian vessels of the Protodynastic and Early Dynastic periods. Apart from affinities the earlier Egyptian Neolithic and Badarian wares have for Nubian pottery traditions, styles of the two lands apparently did not intermingle. The southern advances may have been only an Egyptian colonial presence in order to exploit Nubia's copper and gold and to have access to far southern trading routes. The Nubian material in Egypt suggests a reciprocal immigration of Nubians, whom the Egyptians perhaps employed as mercenaries, as in later times.

So far this essay has concentrated on discussion of the ceramic corpus of Upper Egypt in the Predynastic, but a different local tradition developed in Lower Egypt, where new research and excavation are elucidating the evidence. Pottery at the site of Maadi, near Cairo, was imported from Upper Egypt as early as Naqada I, and local potters copied this import. At Minshat Abu Omar in the eastern Delta, pottery of a thoroughly Upper Egyptian character throughout at least the Naqada II and III of the Predynastic signifies close contact, if not cultural identity, with people from the south. Thus, for much of the fourth millennium B.C., southern Predynastic peoples continued to live side by side with peoples of the indigenous northern cultures of the Delta. Abundant imported foreign pottery, and local copies of it, also characterize both Maadi and Minshat Abu Omar. The road to the East passed directly by Maadi, while Minshat Abu Omar was the last staging post, near the east bank of the Pelusiac branch of the Nile Delta. Protodynastic to Early Dynastic trading encampments have been found between el Arish and el Beda on the north-east road to Palestine, and there was an early Egyptian presence in Canaan. Colonial potters living there used local clays to produce vessels of Egyptian shape as well as vessels following the home traditions.

Arguments for links with southwestern Asia during the Badarian and Amratian are the most tenuous, but a cultural expansion doubtlessly occurred during the Gerzean. The pottery imported from Canaan was copied and adapted. The ledge wavy-handled vessels (Figure 3a) which originated in the early Chalcolithic of Jericho and Beth Shan are

examples. Other Palestinian types, such as bowls with conoid projections below the rim, loop-handled cups and small pots with vertical painted bands, are represented in Egypt by a few examples. The large jars with three or four pierced, triangular lug-handles (Figure 2l) probably link with jars from Iraq, Syria and Iran. The spouted vessels (Figure 3i) were also copied from Mesopotamian prototypes.

In addition to the Delta route, a direct sea route has been postulated between Mesopotamia and Egypt, from the Arabian peninsula up the Red Sea to Upper Egypt (via the Wadi Hammamat). There could also have been a sea route along the Mediterranean coast from Byblos, used to bring resins and wood from Palestine and Syria into Egypt. Modern excavation provides more evidence for a wider trading network from Upper Egypt to the north, east and south in early times than the evidence from as recently as twenty years ago could provide. Modern archaeology is now confirming or refuting the earlier speculations, based on art-historical interpretations of only a few commemorative objects, about this vital formative period.

Pottery was not made primarily for ornament, although aspects of artistic expression obviously developed. Pottery usually served a purpose connected with sustenance, even when placed in the grave. Early Dynastic jar inscriptions indicate that the net-painted cylinders, which evolved from the wavy-handled jars, contained oil (Figure 3j), a precious commodity in the Old Kingdom. The wavy-handled jars found in Gerzean graves (Figure 3c-f) sometimes contain what was perhaps originally aromatic fat, and some of the large storage vessels (Figure 2a,b) have ashes with vegetable paste on the top, perhaps the remains of a funerary feast and libation. Good Nile mud was also used as a substitute commodity for the dead. The international trade was probably concerned with what the jars contained, such as ointments, oils, resins, animal fats and beverages; and the styles were chosen merely for their suitability as containers. Many of the domestic wares would have been used in the preparation and consumption of food and drink. Unfortunately, neither the pillaged graves nor the ruined settlement sites of the Predynastic have produced enough jars with contents which remain sufficiently undecayed for analysis. Often only the "fatty acids" are left from the decomposition of oils and fats in unsealed jars, so identification of the original substances is very difficult; but refined techniques are now making the microanalysis of contents a viable possibility.

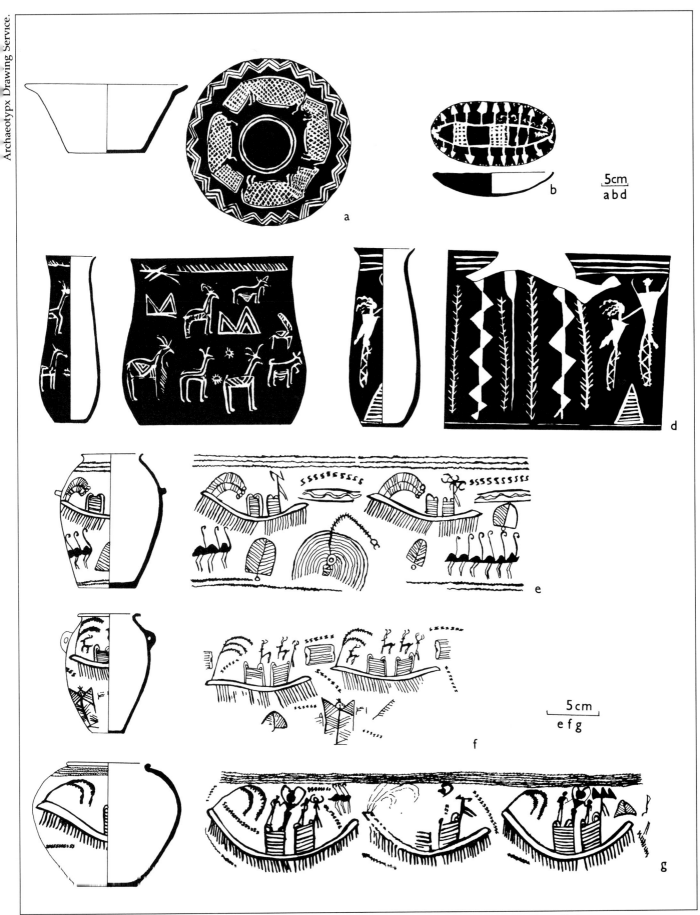

FIGURE 5. Examples of Amratian and Gerzean painted pottery motifs. a-d: C-class; e-g: D-class (after Petrie and Needler).

57

Pottery sherds were also re-used in antiquity. The Badarians obviously prized their rippled bowls; they drilled the edges of broken sherds in order to reconstruct the broken pots by inserting wet thongs and letting them dry to pull the sherds together. Sherds lying about the settlements were picked up and drilled to make spindle whorls, and some of them were sketch pads for early artists. Other sherds were used in construction and as general tools. In the cemeteries, the vandals who came to despoil found that a smashed pot provided a useful selection of digging tools to clear the graves. The sherds so used have bevelled edges, making pottery reconstruction even more difficult.

Appreciation

Apart from the inferences that can be drawn from studying the artifacts, such as pottery, from this early period of Egypt's past, it should not be forgotten that the pottery pieces can also be appreciated in their own right. While little from the Predynastic could be described as a work of art, there is a pleasing simplicity and economy of line in the shapes and decorative devices. Predynastic pots evoke their time and the environment of their making; they are a true gift of the Nile and cannot be mistaken for anything produced elsewhere. In some ways they provide a closer link to the human beings who created them than do the repetitious and often impersonal liturgies inscribed "for eternity" on the later Egyptian monuments.

24. Vase; Gerzean; The University Museum of the University of Pennsylvania (E1340) (Neg. 138876).

DESCRIPTION
OF THE
EXHIBITION
ARTIFACTS

1. Jar; Badarian; The Petrie Museum, University College London (UC 9046).

Predynastic Chronology of Ancient Egypt

Period Name	Approximate Date (B.C.)	Dynasty
(In Egypt)		
Lower Palaeolithic	700,000-90,000	
Middle Palaeolithic	90,000-28,000	
Late Palaeolithic	28,000-8000	
Epipalaeolithic	8000-6000/5500	
Neolithic	8000/6000-4000	
Badarian	5500/4000-3800	
Amratian (Naqada I)	3800-3500/3400	
Gerzean (Naqada II)	3500/3400-3200	
Protodynastic (Naqada III)	3200-3100	

Dynastic Chronology of Ancient Egypt

Archaic Period	3100-2700	I and II
Old Kingdom	2700-2230	III-VI
First Intermediate Period	2230-2050	VII-X
Middle Kingdom	2050-1750	XI-XII
Second Intermediate Period	1750-1552	XIII-XVII
New Kingdom	1552-1080	XVIII-XX
Third Intermediate Period	1080-664	XXI-XXV
Saite Period	664-525	XXVI
Late Period	525-332	XXVII-XXXI
Ptolemaic Period	332-31	XXXII

1. Jar

Badari Tomb 5112
Rippled Ware
Badarian
Ht: 12.5 cm (4 15/16 in.)
The Petrie Museum, University College London
(UC 9046)

A rippled and burnished surface characterizes this style of thin-walled cylindrical jar. This vessel is the oldest example of pottery in the exhibition and exemplifies the refinement of the ceramic art already achieved by earliest Predynastic (Badarian) times.

2. Bowl

Naqada and Ballas
Plum Red Ware
Probable Amratian
Ht: 8.0 cm x Diam: 17.0 cm (3 1/4 in. x 6 3/4 in.)
The Charleston Museum, South Carolina (ARM 11)

Plum Red Ware bowls are found in tombs and settlements and thus provide a way to compare and date different types of Predynastic sites.

3. Vase

Provenance unknown, purchased in Luxor
Black-Topped Plum Red Ware
Amratian
Ht: 15.8 cm x Diam: 15.8 cm (6 1/8 in. x 6 1/8 in.)
Royal Ontario Museum, Toronto (900.2.7)

This vase has a simple everted lip and a wide mouth; its slightly convex sides taper to a flat circular base. A "T"-shaped pot mark is inscribed on base. The "T" sign may be a maker's mark and is thought by some to foreshadow hieroglyphic writing.

4. Necked Vase

Provenance unknown
Plum Red Ware (white cross-lined painted)
Amratian
Ht: 32.0 cm x Diam: 11.2 cm (12 3/4 in. x 3 11/16 in.)
Royal Ontario Museum, Toronto (910.85.88)

Plum Red Ware decorated with painted white/cream motifs. Lower body is slightly bulbous while the upper portion tapers to a long neck and terminates in a flaring lip. Decoration consists of a lower band, 6.4 cm thick, of

9. Bowl; The Petrie Museum, University College London (UC 15337).

lattice above which three plant forms appear on one side of the neck while various animals enliven the other. Slip has been badly worn. The interior lip has been decorated with radiating lines.

5. Vase

Provenance unknown
Black-Topped Plum Red Ware
Amratian
Ht: 9.0 cm x Diam: 23.0 cm (3 35/64 in. x 8 in.)
(c) 1987 The Detroit Institute of Arts (79.44.1)
Founders Society Purchase, Acquisitions Fund

This black-topped vase with everted lip and wide mouth has a red burnished body and comes from Tomb Group (58).

6. Double Vase

Provenance unknown, purchased in Luxor
Black-Topped Plum Red Ware
Amratian
Ht: 17.8 cm x Diam: 8.2 cm (7 in. x 3 1/4 in.)
Royal Ontario Museum, Toronto (900.2.9)

Two black-topped roughly cylindrical vases taper gently to a solid horizontal tube, which connects both vessels. One vase is slightly larger than the other. The form recalls the upraised arms of the "ka" sign and probably had magical significance. Minor damage to one vase.

7. Double Jar

Provenance unknown, purchased in Luxor
Plum Red Ware
Amratian
Ht: 19.6 cm x Diam: 2.2 cm (7 3/4 in. x 1 11/16 in.)
Royal Ontario Museum, Toronto (900.2.11)

Thought possibly to be a yogurt maker, this double vase is made of coarse brown-ocher clay that has been burnished red. The two ovoid jars converge into a single, long slender neck. Each jar has a flattened oblique base. Minor damage to the rim.

8. Bowl

Provenance unknown, purchased in Luxor
Plum Red Ware (white cross-lined painted)
Amratian
Ht: 7.0 cm x Diam: 19.4 cm (2 3/4 in. x 7 3/4 in.)
Royal Ontario Museum, Toronto (900.2.17)

This bowl is of red-brown slipped and burnished clay decorated with a white/cream paint. Decorations appear on the interior and the exterior. Internally, chevrons are placed close to one another while the exterior has an outside ring of solid triangles alternating above and below a line parallel to the rim. Bowl has had damage and is repaired.

12. Vase; Amratian-Gerzean; Royal Ontario Museum, Toronto (918.32.5).

9. Bowl

Provenance unknown, Flinders Petrie purchase
Plum Red Ware (white cross-lined painted)
Amratian
Diam: 15.0 cm (5 7/8 in.)
The Petrie Museum, University College London
(UC 15337)

This shallow bowl is decorated in the white cross-lined style with hippopotami which encircle the upper interior wall near the rim of the shallow bowl. Bowl has been broken and partially repaired.

10. Dish

Provenance unknown, purchased in Luxor
Plum Red Ware (white cross-lined painted)
Amratian
Ht: 6.6 cm x Lth: 27.6 cm x Wth: 19.4 cm (2 5/8 in. x 10 15/16 in. x 7 5/8 in.)
Royal Ontario Museum, Toronto (900.2.103)

The interior of this oval, Plum Red Ware dish is decorated with angular sketches of giraffe-like animals which are applied in white pigment. Black smears occur on the sides and base. Minor damage.

11. Jar

el'Adaima (Adaima no. 32)
Basalt
Amratian-Gerzean
Ht: 28.9 cm (11 3/8 in.)
The Brooklyn Museum, (07.447.187)
Museum Collection Fund

This cylindrical jar has been deeply hollowed to within 4.0 cm from the bottom. The pronounced drill marks on the interior are characteristic of early basalt vessels. Two narrow string-hole handles occur on either side.

12. Vase

Provenance unknown, purchased piece
Black-Topped Plum Red Ware
Amratian-Gerzean
Ht: 25.1 cm x Diam: 11.8 cm (9 1/2 in. x 4 5/8 in.)
Royal Ontario Museum, Toronto (918.32.5)

This vase is made of brown Nile clay. A band between the red body and blackened top has a brown-ocher tone from the process of refiring used to obtain the black top effect. The vessel is a truncated conical form with convex sides. A design suggesting a building or enclosure has been roughly scratched into the vase after it was fired. Minor damage at rim.

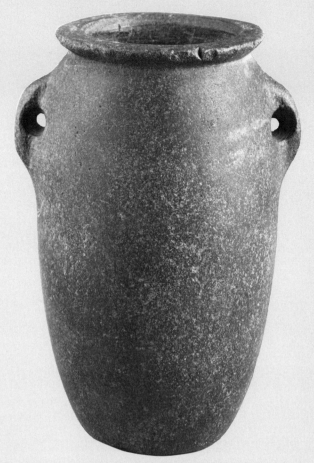

13. Stone Vase; Amratian-Gerzean; Royal Ontario Museum, Toronto (900.2.140).

13. Stone Vase

Provenance unknown, purchased in Luxor
Basalt
Amratian-Gerzean
Ht: 19.0 cm x Diam: 10.2 cm (7 1/2 in. x 4 in.)
Royal Ontario Museum, Toronto (900.2.140)

This oval vase is made from speckled black and brown basalt. The vessel is typical of earlier Predynastic shapes. It features a flat base, a flared mouth with flat rim and two perforated handles at the shoulder. Minor damage.

14. Jar

Naqada
Black-Topped Plum Red Ware
Late Amratian-Gerzean
Ht: 37.0 cm (14 5/8 in.)
The University Museum, University of Pennsylvania (E-14383)

This ovoid black-topped burnished red ware jar has a wide mouth.

16. Bowl with Human-like Feet; Gerzean; Royal Ontario Museum, Toronto (900.2.128).

15. Duck-Shaped Vase

Provenance unknown, Flinders Petrie Purchase
Earthenware
Gerzean
Lth: 15.8 cm (6 1/4 in.)
The Petrie Museum, University College London
(UC 15353)

Shaping vases in the form of animals was a popular Egyptian practice and such vases, whether carved from stone or made from clay, are formally called theriomorphic vases and classified by Flinders Petrie as "Fancy ware."

16. Bowl with Human-like Feet

Provenance unknown, purchased in Luxor
Coarse Ware
Gerzean
Ht: 7.9 cm x Diam: 14.7 cm (3 1/8 in. x 5 3/4 in.)
Royal Ontario Museum, Toronto (900.2.128)

This shallow bowl with slightly everted lip and flat base has been coated and burnished with the characteristic red slip. The bowl tips forward and rests on two human-like feet. Minor damage and repair.

17. Jar

Hierakonpolis Fort Cemetery 59
Earthenware
Gerzean
Ht: 11.1 cm x Diam: 8.4 cm (4 3/8 in. x 3 5/16 in.)
The Oriental Institute, University of Chicago
(OIM 29837)

This jar is typical of Gerzean tomb groups and exemplifies the Hierakonpolis pottery industry. The oval body of the jar extends to a short neck terminating in a flared mouth.

18. Vase

Naqada and Ballas
Black-Topped Plum Red Ware
Gerzean
Ht: 12.0 cm x Largest Cir: 38.0 cm x Diam. of opening: 5.5 cm (7 1/8 in. x 15 in. x 2 1/4 in.)
The Charleston Museum, South Carolina (ARM 30)

This globular black-topped red ware vase has a rounded bottom, a slightly pointed and rolled rim and may have been used for offerings of milk. A narrow brown-ocher colored zone between the red body and black top resulted from secondary firing of the pot, mouth down, to produce the distinctive blackening around its rim.

19. Hanging Vase

Abydos
Diorite
Gerzean
Ht: 13.3 cm x Diam: 5.0 cm (5 1/4 in. x 2 in.)
Royal Ontario Museum, Toronto (908.40.1)

This vase of mottled black and white diorite has a neck which has been covered in gold foil. The egg-shaped vessel has perforated roll handles and a sloping neck extending into a rim. Extensive restoration.

20. Roll Rim Jar

Provenance unknown
Plum Red Ware
Gerzean
Ht: 25.8 cm x Diam: 18.3 cm (10 1/8 in. x 7 1/4 in.)
The Charleston Museum, South Carolina
(ARM 322)

This vase is made of brown Nile clay covered with a plum red slip. Oval in shape, the vase has a narrow base and flares to a short, prominently shaped roll rim typical of the Gerzean period.

21. Vessel

Hierakonpolis Fort Cemetery 26
Earthenware
Gerzean
Ht: 20.1 cm x Diam: 13.1 cm (7 15/16 in. x 5 3/16 in.)
The Oriental Institute, University of Chicago
(OIM 29874)

This ovoid jar has an everted rim with two string hole handles. Encircling the jar are wavy lines which become dots and then straight lines near the bottom of the jar.

22. Bowl

Hierakonpolis Fort Cemetery 26
Plum Red Ware
Gerzean
Ht: 7.9 cm x Diam: 17.5 cm (3 1/16 in. x 6 7/8 in.)
The Oriental Institute, University of Chicago
(OIM 29824)

This "half-polished bowl" is smooth and compact with a flat base and flaring sides. The interior has been coated with a pink-red wash of slip which extends over the rim to the upper portion of the exterior and has been burnished. This "half-polished" decorative technique is characteristic of the Gerzean period.

17. Jar; Gerzean; Courtesy of The Oriental Institute of The University of Chicago (OIM 29837) (P.6755/N.46431).

20. Roll Rim Jar; Gerzean; The Charleston Museum, South Carolina (ARM 322).

21. Vessel; Gerzean; Courtesy of The Oriental Institute of The University of Chicago (OIM 29874) (P.67660/N.46436).

22. Bowl; Gerzean; The Oriental Institute of The University of Chicago (OIM 29824) (P.67651/N.46427).

23. Vase

Provenance unknown, purchased piece
Black-Topped Plum Red Ware
Gerzean
Ht: 39.6 cm x Diam: 13.9 cm (15 5/8 in. x 5 1/2 in.)
Royal Ontario Museum, Toronto (918.32.4)

This tall black-top conical vase contracts slightly below the rim. Body has been broken longitudinally and repaired.

24. Vase

Naqada and Ballas
Breccia
Gerzean
Ht: 7.3 cm x Wth: 2.6 cm (2 7/8 in. x 1 1/16 in.)
The University Museum, University of Pennsylvania (E-1340)

This egg-shaped vase made of alabaster breccia with two tubular side handles shows evidence of minor damage to its flaring, flat-top lip.

25. Roll Rim Jar

Provenance unknown, Flinders Petrie purchase
Buff Ware
Middle Gerzean
Ht: 42.0 cm (16 1/2 in.)
The Petrie Museum, University College London (UC 6340)

Red painted boats, long-legged birds (ostriches or flamingos), crocodiles and wavy lines decorate the exterior surface of this earthenware jar. The boats depicted on this jar are similar to those found on paintings and in relief in the tombs of the period. Slightly raised handles appear on either side of the jar. This is one of the largest decorated Gerzean pots in existence.

26. Jar

Provenance unknown, purchased in Egypt
Buff Ware
Middle Gerzean
Ht: 22.0 cm x Diam: 11.3 cm (8 5/8 in. x 4 7/16 in.)
Royal Ontario Museum, Toronto (910.85.79)

This jar of buff-colored clay, has decoration painted in red and sits on an unsteady circular base. The vase is an ovoid form with contracted mouth and thick inverted rim. Perforated barrel-shaped handles occur on either side. Decoration is identical on the two faces. A galley with two cabins and a prow standard appears on each face; "ssss" shapes indicate water, and large plants are painted under the handles and the boat. Wavy lines encircle the base.

27. Roll Rim Jar

Provenance unknown, purchased piece
Buff Ware
Middle Gerzean
Ht: 25.1 cm x Diam: 11.3 cm (9 7/8 in. x 4 7/16 in.)
Royal Ontario Museum, Toronto (918.32.3)

This buff-colored clay jar is egg-shaped with a contracted mouth and low rolled rim. The vessel is decorated in red-ocher paint with designs of three boats, antelopes and plants. Excellent condition.

28. Jar

Provenance unknown, Flinders Petrie purchase
Earthenware
Middle Gerzean
Ht: 17.5 cm (6 15/16 in.)
The Petrie Museum, University College London (UC 10702)

Decorated with a spiral design, this jar is squat with two protruding handles and rolled rim. According to Petrie, this type of vessel appears to be a part of the decorated pot family; however, it does not have the familiar antelopes, ostriches and boats.

29. Jar with Animal Face

Provenance unknown
Serpentine
Middle-Late Gerzean
Ht: 3.0 cm (1 3/16 in.)
The Detroit Institute of Arts (90.1S12964)
Gift of Frederick K. Stearns

This small jar with face of an animal protruding from one side probably portrays a baboon, bear or dog. The squat shape, barrel handles and flattened rim are typical of Gerzean vases.

30. Wavy-Handled Jar

Provenance unknown
Buff Ware
Late Gerzean
Ht: 22.7 cm (8 7/8 in.)
The University Museum, University of Pennsylvania (E-1645)

Starting at the flat base the sides of this jar rise to form high sloping shoulders which terminate in a short neck with a rolled rim. The two wavy handles found on the jar's shoulders are useful for dating purposes and show kinship with Palestinian jars.

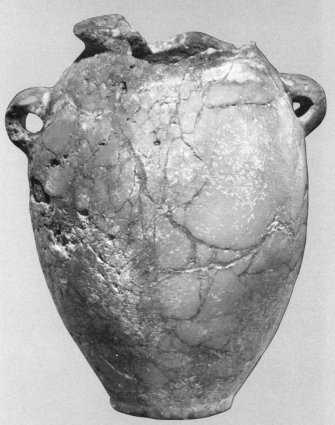

24. Vase; Gerzean; The University Museum of The University of Pennsylvania (E-1340) (Neg. 138876).

25. Roll Rim Jar; Middle Gerzean; The Petrie Museum, University College London (UC 6340).

26. Jar; Middle Gerzean; Royal Ontario Museum, Toronto (910.85.79).

27. Roll Rim Jar; Middle Gerzean; Royal Ontario Museum, Toronto (918.32.3).

30. Wavy-Handled Jar; Late Gerzean; The University Museum of The University of Pennsylvania (E-1645).

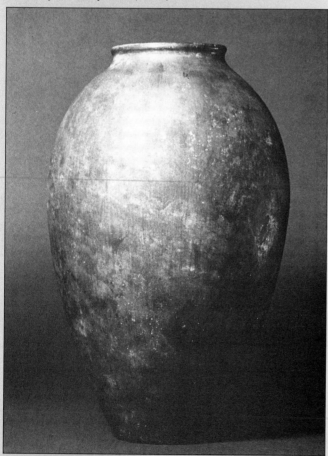

31. Roll Rim Jar; Late Gerzean; The University Museum of The University of Pennsylvania (E-1816).

31. Roll Rim Jar

Naqada (Cemetery A) or Ballas (Cemetery C)
Grave 489
Plum Red Ware
Late Gerzean
Ht: 31.7 cm x Diam: 20.3 cm (12 1/2 in. x 7 1/32 in.)
The University Museum, University of
Pennsylvania (E-1816)

This ovoid Plum Red Ware jar has a flat base, a short neck and a rolled rim.

32. Jar

Provenance unknown
Red Ware
Late Gerzean
Ht: 15.4 cm (6 1/16 in.)
The University Museum, University of
Pennsylvania (E-1395)

This egg-shaped light red ware body rests on a flat base. It is decorated with groups of wavy horizontal lines and four bands of wavy lines encircle the rim in red paint. The lines may be a copy of twisted rush work.

33. Jar

el Ma'mariya (Ma'mariya no. 30)
Plum Red Ware (Red-polished)
Gerzean-Early Protodynastic (Naqada II-Early Naqada III)
Ht: 25.9 cm (10 1/4 in.)
The Brooklyn Museum, (07.447.349)
Museum Collection Fund

Jars of this type have been found in graves of the Naqada II and early Naqada III periods. This body has convex sides which extend to a separately made and attached neck.

34. Jar

Naqada and Ballas
Plum Red Ware
Gerzean-Protodynastic
Ht: 11.0 cm x Cir: 32.0 cm x Diam: 4.0 cm (4 5/16 in. x 12 5/8 in. x 1 3/4 in.)
The Charleston Museum, South Carolina (ARM 39)

This globular jar has a burnished red surface and short neck.

35. Fish-Shaped Pot

Provenance unknown, Flinders Petrie purchase
Earthenware
Gerzean-Protodynastic
Ht: 9.5 cm (3 3/4 in.)
The Petrie Museum, University College London (UC 2965)

This black-topped brown pot shaped in the form of a fish

has a wide mouth on the side. The eyes are detailed by incised lines, and slight depressions form the gills of the fish. Fish shapes and images were used in a variety of objects. Fish-shaped palettes were common and fish often decorated the earlier white cross-lined pottery.

36. Vase

Provenance unknown
Alabaster
Gerzean-Protodynastic
Ht: 12.4 cm x Cir: 7.7 cm (4 7/8 in. x 3 1/16 in.)
The University Museum, University of
Pennsylvania (E-1349)

This small alabaster vase sits on a flat base and rises to high sloping shoulders which terminate in a rolled rim. This style mimics a pottery type of the time. Small stone jars were often used in tombs to hold oils and ointments for the afterlife.

37. Frog-Shaped Vase

Provenance unknown, purchased in Egypt
Serpentine
Gerzean-Protodynastic
Ht: 5.0 cm x Lth: 7.6 cm (1 3/8 in. x 3 in.)
Royal Ontario Museum, Toronto (910.100.3)

The serpentine vase is carved in the shape of a frog with bulging body and protruding eyes. It has a small round opening in the top with low rim. Pierced horizontal roll handles are carved into the sides. Minor damage.

38. Roll Rim Jar

Naqada (Cemetery A) or Ballas (Cemetery C)
Grave 284
Earthenware with Cream Slip
Protodynastic
Ht: 23.5 cm (9 1/4 in.)
The University Museum, University of
Pennsylvania (E-1653)

This light red ware vessel is decorated with a wavy band of cream slip painted around the neck. Cylindrical vase has a flat base and is topped by a rolled rim.

39. Bowl

Naqada (Cemetery A) or Ballas (Cemetery C)
Grave 92
Plum Red Ware
Protodynastic
Diam: 26.5 cm (10 7/16 in.)
The University Museum, University of
Pennsylvania (E-1556)

This light red ware bowl has been coarsely burnished in parallel lines. Bowl is shallow and sits on a flat base.

35. Fish-Shaped Pot; Gerzean-Protodynastic; The Petrie Museum, University College London (UC 2965).

38. Roll Rim Jar; Protodynastic; The University Museum of The University of Pennsylvania (E-1653).

41. Bowl; Protodynastic; The University Museum of The University of Pennsylvania (E-1696) (Neg. 138880).

40. Wavy-Handled Jar

Abu Zaiden (Abu Zaiden no.69)
Serpentine
Protodynastic (Naqada III)
Ht: 14.1 cm (5 9/16 in.)
The Brooklyn Museum, (09.889.31)
Museum Collection Fund

This vessel reflects the influence of wavy-handled pottery of Naqada II and the beginning of Naqada III; however, the handles on this jar have been pierced with two vertical string holes. The jar is hollow to 1.5 cm from the bottom.

41. Bowl

Naqada (Cemetery A) or Ballas (Cemetery C)
Grave 100
Coarse Ware
Protodynastic
Ht: 26.7 cm (10 7/16 in.)
The University Museum, University of Pennsylvania (E-1696)

This hat-shaped bowl has a flat base and flaring rim and is typical of the Protodynastic period.

42. Roll Rim Storage Jar

Abydos
Plum Red Ware
Protodynastic
Ht: 62.2 cm x Diam: 34.0 cm (24 1/2 in. x 13 3/8 in.)
Royal Ontario Museum, Toronto (901.8.1)

This Plum Red Ware storage jar has almost straight sides that taper from rounded shoulders to a pointed base. It has a small mouth with a rolled rim that is flattened slightly at the top and on the outside. There are vertical shaping marks on the body of the jar. The remains of a sticky substance, probably remains of the jar's original contents, cover the interior. Mouth and body of jar have been badly scarred.

43. Bowl inscribed with the name Scorpion

Hierakonpolis Main Deposit
Calcite (alabaster)
Protodynastic
Ht: 3.6 cm (1 7/16 in.)
The Petrie Museum, University College London (UC 14953)

Calcite (alabaster) bowl with flattened base curving at the edge. The rim is chipped in places, is not symmetrical, and gives the effect of a non-rigid prototype of a pot or a basket. An interior circular incised line is slightly off-center, while a circular incised depression marks the true center. The surface is smooth and banded in brown, grey and white. Just below the exterior rim, an incised inscription is filled with blue paint. Two sets of joined arms, inverted over a "t" or "r" sign in front of a scorpion with tail, comprise the inscription. King Scorpion is also known from his magnificent ceremonial macehead found at Hierakonpolis.

44. Bowl inscribed with the name Irj-Hor

Hierakonpolis Main Deposit
Calcite (alabaster)
Protodynastic
Ht: 4.8 cm (1 7/8 in.)
The Petrie Museum, University College London
(UC 14962)

This almost hemispherically-shaped alabaster bowl sits on a slightly flattened base. A narrow rim is incised with four groups of lines encircling it at almost equal distance from one another. There are five lines in each group; on the exterior, they terminate just above the base level of the interior set. In the center of two of these groups is an inscription inlaid with blue pigment; the inscription is formed by two joined arms with hands inverted over a "t" or "r" sign in front of a bird with a long rectangular tail which is carved over an upturned crescent. The surface of the bowl is smooth and banded in cream, white, orange and buff. Irj-Hor is believed to have been a late Protodynastic King and is known from Abydos. Earlier sources transcribed his name as "Ro."

45. Jar

Provenance unknown
Buff ware
Protodynastic
Ht: 17.5 cm x Diam: 12.5 cm (6 7/8 in. x 4 7/8 in.)
Royal Ontario Museum, Toronto (910.85.190)

This buff ware jar sits on a flat base with convex sides rising to a short neck and roll rim. It is painted on the shoulder with groups of four red wavy lines and oblique lines are roughly incised on the neck.

46. Jar inscribed with the name Hor-Aha ca. 3100-3050

Provenance unknown
Alabaster
Early Dynasty I
Ht: 33.02 cm (13 in.)
The Detroit Institute of Arts (71.400)
Founders Society Purchase, Ancient Art Fund

This straight-sided cylindrical alabaster jar rests on a flat base. Below the rolled rim is a narrow rope decoration. The shape and decoration of this vase is paralleled by ceramic pots of this period commonly used for tomb offerings. The name of the king "Aha" is imprinted into the upper center portion of the jar. As is traditional, the king's name is surmounted by the hawk representing the god Horus, a patron deity of early kings, and sits above a

43. Bowl inscribed with the name Scorpion; Protodynastic; The Petrie Museum, University College London (UC 14953).

44. Bowl inscribed with the name Irj-Hor; Protodynastic; The Petrie Museum, University College London (UC 14962).

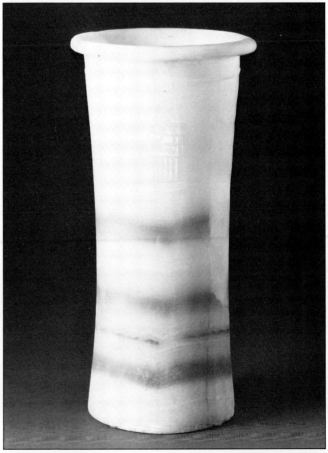

46. Jar inscribed with the name of Hor-Aha ca. 3100-3050 B.C.; Early Dynasty I; (c) 1987 The Detroit Institute of Arts, Founders Society Purchase, Ancient Art Fund (71.400).

47. Bowl; Dynasty I (Archaic); Royal Ontario Museum, Ontario (909.80.123).

stylized niched or "serekh" palace facade. This "Horus name" of the king—one of three titles in Archaic times—may be read "the Horus" or simply, "Hor-Aha." Some restoration has been done. Shape of this jar is similar to (38).

47. Bowl

Provenance unknown, purchased in Egypt
Slate
Dynasty I (Archaic)
Ht: 9.6 cm x Diam: 34.6 cm (3 3/8 in. x 13 5/8 in.)
Royal Ontario Museum, Toronto (909.80.123)

This shallow bowl of dark grey-green slate has an interiorly incised circular base and rim.

48. Dish

Abydos, Umm el-Ga'ab, Tomb of Semerkhet ca. 2950 B.C.
Calcite
Dynasty I (Archaic)
Diam: 42.0 cm (16 9/16 in.)
The Petrie Museum, University College London (UC 17539)

This circular dish with a rolled rim is unusually large and shallow. Stone vessel manufacture reached a peak during the Archaic period.

49. Nedod Jar Fragment

Abydos Umm el-Ga'ab, Tomb of King Semerkhet ca. 2950 B.C.
Earthenware
Dynasty I (Archaic)
Ht: 19.5 cm (7 3/4 in.)
The University Museum, University of Pennsylvania (E 6861-A)

This fragment indicates that the jar was a typical Syrian shape. The long neck and bulbous body differ from typical Egyptian shapes. Foreign trade peaked at the end of the Predynastic and by Archaic times had become a royal monopoly.

50. Bowl Fragment inscribed with the names Den and Enezib

Abydos, Umm el-Ga'ab, exact provenance uncertain
Rock Crystal
Dynasty I (Archaic)
Ht: 6.6 cm (2 5/8 in.)
The University Museum, University of Pennsylvania (E 6847)

This rock crystal fragment of a bowl is inscribed with the king names Den and Enezib (Anedjib) of Dynasty I. Royal names on a stone vase may indicate it was an offering to a king or kings or to their spirits or that the vessel might have been a gift from him to reward a loyal client.

51. Vase

Lahoun
Alabaster
Dynasty I (Archaic)
Ht: 8.0 cm x Cir: 23.0 cm x Diam: 5.0 cm (3 1/4 in. x 9 in. x 2 in.)
The Charleston Museum, South Carolina (ARM 14)

This rounded alabaster jar has a slight everted lip at the top. Jars of this nature were often placed in the tombs for storage of oils and ointments. During Predynastic times, the jars were functional; later, they were purely decorative since they often were not hollowed out.

52. Bowl

Sedment
Slate
Dynasty II (Archaic)
Ht: 17.5 cm x Diam: 7.2 cm (6 7/8 in. x 2 7/8 in.)
The Charleston Museum, South Carolina (ARM 238)

This grey-green slate bowl has a lipped rim and angular shoulder. Some restoration has been done. Shapes like this often reflect metal (copper) prototypes in Archaic times.

53. Saucer

Provenance unknown
Limestone
Dynasties I-II (Archaic)
Ht: 2.8 cm x Diam: 11.0 cm (1 1/16 in. x 4 3/8 in.)
The Brooklyn Museum, (09.889.29)
Museum Fund Collection

This saucer of pink limestone has a plain horizontal rim. A smaller saucer of similar shape and stone was found at Abu Zaidan (near Hierakonpolis) by the Henri de Morgan expedition.

54. Bowl

Nubia
Earthenware
Dynasty XI or XII, Nubian C (Middle Kingdom)
Ht: 7.6 cm x Diam: 8.6 cm (2 15/16 in. x 3 3/8 in.)
Royal Ontario Museum, Toronto (900.2.91)

Gourd-shaped bowl made of dark clay that has been burnished and fired black. It sits on a round base and is decorated with oblique lines incised in a lattice pattern which has been filled with white slip. The incised decoration on this pot typifies a Nubian and Saharan ceramic tradition which both predates and survives that of Predynastic Egypt. Its influence is reflected in incised Predynastic pottery. There is some damage which has been repaired.

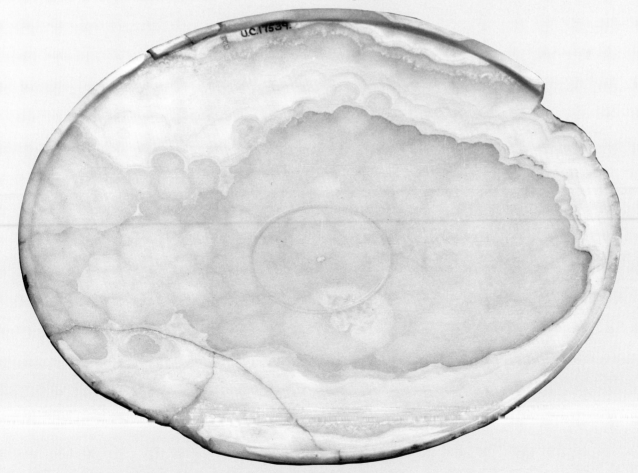

48. Dish; Dynasty I (Archaic); The Petrie Museum, University College London (UC 17539).

55. Bucrania or Bull Head
Palette; Amratian; Royal
Ontario Museum,
Ontario (900.2.52).

55. Bucrania or Bull Head Palette

Provenance unknown, purchased in Luxor
Slate
Amratian
Lth: 61.0 cm x Wth: 36.6 cm (17 5/8 in. x 4 3/4 in.)
Royal Ontario Museum, Toronto (900.2.52)

This green-grey palette is lozenge-shaped, with slightly convex faces. One end has an ornamental bull or cow head with projecting horns. One horn is broken. Brownish stains are present on one face, possibly indicating the preparation of hematite-based pigment.

56. Palette

Purchased in Luxor
Slate
Amratian
Lth: 38.4 cm x Wth: 18.7 cm (15 1/8 in. x 7 3/8 in.)
Royal Ontario Museum, Toronto (900.2.54)

This lozenge-shaped green slate palette is rounded at the sides and on the narrow end. The broader end of the palette has five strong indentations and hook-like projections at each corner. Some minor damage.

58. Tomb Group; (c) 1987 The Detroit Institute of Arts, Founders Society Purchase, Acquisitions Fund (79.44.1, 79.44.3-79.44.14, 79.44.16-79.44.23).

57. Bracelet

Provenance unknown
Copper
Amratian
Diam: 6.8 cm (2 43/64 in.)
The Detroit Institute of Arts (79.44.13)
Founders Society Purchase, Acquisitions Fund

This copper bracelet is part of Tomb Group (58). It appears to have a raised decoration on one side. The bracelet was placed in the tomb with other objects for the deceased. Copper was very rare in Amratian times and was usually one of the first materials plundered from a tomb.

58. Tomb Group (group of 21)

Provenance unknown
Flint, copper, shell, mica and Black-Topped Plum Red Ware
Amratian
The Detroit Institute of Arts (79.44.1, 79.44.3 - 79.44.14, 79.44.16 - 79.44.23)
Founders Society Purchase, Acquisitions Fund

Included in the group are copper (57) and shell bracelets, rings, worked shells, a vase (5), a sheet of mica, flint tools and a crude slate palette. All of these objects were placed in the tomb for the use of the deceased in the afterlife. The Amratian date of this group is indicated by the carinated bowl and black-topped vase.

59. Handled Comb; Amratian-early Gerzean; Royal Ontario Museum, Toronto (910.85.5).

59. Handled Comb

Provenance unknown, purchased in Egypt
Ivory
Amratian-early Gerzean
Lth: 8.8 cm x Wth: 2.7 cm (3 9/16 in. x 1 1/16 in.)
Royal Ontario Museum, Toronto (910.85.5)

Two birds are carved into the top of the ivory comb, both of which have long necks and no tails. The beak of the bird on the right has been broken off. Three short teeth remain in the comb's body while five teeth are missing.

60. Disc-Shaped Macehead

el'Adaima (Adaima no. 43)
Porphyry
Amratian-Gerzean (Naqada II-Naqada III)
Ht: 2.4 cm x Diam: 9.1 cm (15/16 in. x 3 5/8 in.)
The Brooklyn Museum, (07.447.873)
Museum Collection Fund

Made of black and white diorite porphyry, the macehead has a slightly concave top with a sharp edge. This shape probably developed through an evolution from a wooden club which was attached by a withe or cord to a handle. Maceheads were usually fitted to a haft.

61. Biconical Macehead

Upper Egypt (purchased)
Breccia
Amratian-Gerzean
Lth: 19.7 cm x Wth: 5 cm (7 3/4 in. x 2 in.)
Royal Ontario Museum, Toronto (909.80.43)

This red breccia macehead is a long biconical form. One tip is beveled on lower side and the other tip has been broken off. The surfaces are scarred and pitted slightly. The rare shape is thought to represent a transitional stage between disk and pear-shaped styles of maceheads.

62. Pendants

Naqada (Cemetery A) or Ballas (Cemetery C)
Grave 132
Ivory
Amratian-Gerzean
each: Ht: 6.7 cm (2 5/8 in.)
The University Museum, University of
Pennsylvania (E-1174)

Two ivory pendants are shaped like arrows and have incised decorative lines. They probably fulfilled magical functions.

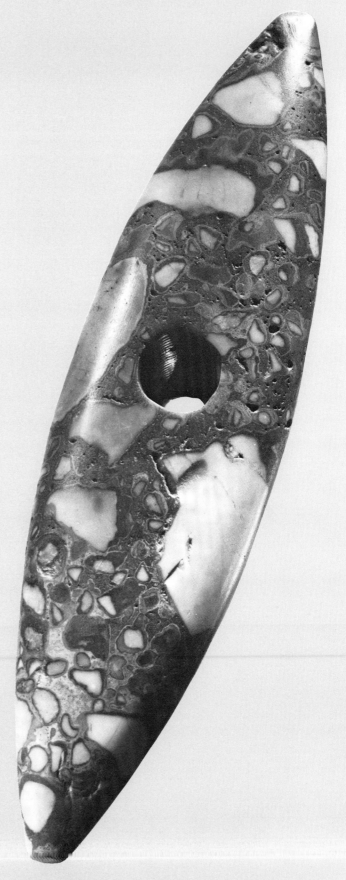

61. Biconical Macehead; Amratian-Gerzean; Royal Ontario Museum, Toronto (909.80.43).

62. Pendant; Amratian-Gerzean; The University Museum of The University of Pennsylvania (E-1174) (Neg. 138871).

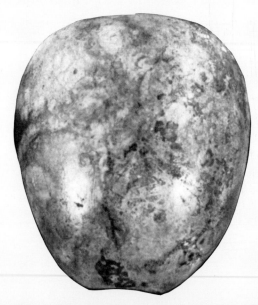

63. Pear-Shaped Macehead; Gerzean; Courtesy of The Oriental Institute of The University of Chicago (OIM 18263) (P.67650/N.46426).

63. Pear-Shaped Macehead

Provenance unknown
Stone
Gerzean
Ht: 5.6 cm x Diam: 5.0 cm (2 1/4 in. x 2 in.)
The Oriental Institute, University of Chicago
(OIM 18263)

The pear-shaped macehead is of mottled stone and is perforated vertically. Maceheads symbolized the power of the chief or king and were primarily ceremonial.

64. Fish-Shaped Palette

Naqada-Tomb T 1656
Slate
Gerzean
Lth: 14.1 cm x Wth: 10.1 cm (5 9/16 in. x 4 in.)
The Oriental Institute, University of Chicago
(OIM 881)

This fish-shaped palette has a large oval body and a small triangular tail. There is an indication of an incised line on the front of the palette. The shape reflects the domination of the Nile on everyday life.

65. Double Bird Head Palette

el Amrah, B 129
Slate
Gerzean
Lth: 19.3 cm x Wth: 10.1 cm (7 5/8 in. x 4 in.)
The University Museum, University of
Pennsylvania (E-9600)

This slate palette is surmounted with two facing bird heads. Palettes such as these were originally used to grind malachite and hematite pigments for eye cosmetics. Centuries later, they were also used as ceremonial or commemorative plaques.

66. Bird Head Hair Ornament

Provenance unknown
Ivory
Gerzean
Ht: 9.1 cm (3 9/16 in.)
The University Museum, University of
Pennsylvania (E-1139)

The needle-shaped hair ornament is decorated with incised lines and surmounted by the head of a bird.

67. Model House

Provenance unknown, purchased in Luxor
Pink-Buff Clay
Gerzean
Ht: 25.1 cm x Lth: 38.7 cm x Wth: 22.9 cm (9 7/8 in. x 15 1/4 in. x 9 in.)
Royal Ontario Museum, Toronto (900.2.45)

Model houses were sometimes placed in Predynastic tombs to provide the soul with a home for the afterlife.

64. Fish-Shaped Palette; Gerzean; Courtesy of The Oriental Institute of The University of Chicago (OIM 881) (P.676382/N.464143).

65. Double Bird Head Palette; Gerzean; The University Museum of The University of Pennsylvania (E-9600).

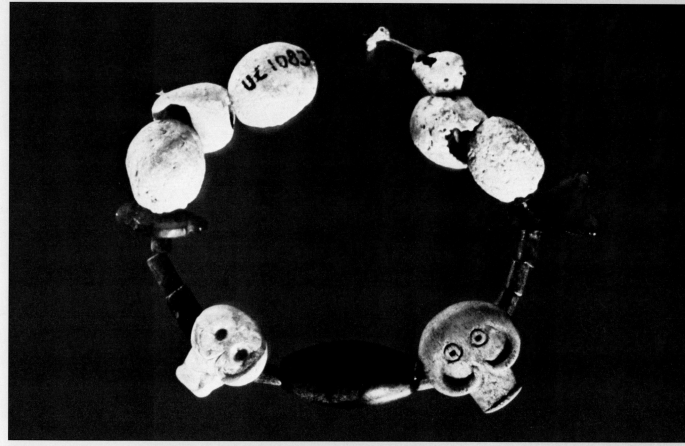

70. Necklace; Gerzean-Protodynastic; The Petrie Museum, University College London (UC 10834-8).

The practice of providing a "soul house" substantially increased in Dynastic times. This house is of pink-buff clay with dark red incised designs. The floor plan is rectangular and has an arched roof with a center pole ridge extending along the crown. One opening is on a side and a smaller, circular opening is at the top. Incised and painted animals similar to those on Gerzean pots decorate one end of the house and incised circles occur on the other faces. This house is a unique Predynastic example both in shape and decoration. In addition to modern restoration, there is evidence of ancient redecoration.

68. Double Bird Head Palette

Said to come from Gebelein
Schist
Late Gerzean-Protodynastic (Late Naqada II-Naqada III)
Ht: 29.5 cm (11 5/8 in.)
The Brooklyn Museum, (16.580.126)
Gift of the Estate of Charles Edwin Wilbour
through Mrs. Evangeline Wilbour Blashfield

This lozenge-shaped palette is topped by two stylized bird heads (possibly hawks). The eyes of both faces are lined with beads of ostrich shell and filled with black paste. The beak of one bird is missing. The double bird palette shape survived into the Naqada III.

69. Pear-Shaped Macehead

Provenance unknown
Diorite
Gerzean-Protodynastic
Ht: 4.0 cm x Diam: 4.4 cm (1 9/16 in. x 1 3/4 in.)
The Oriental Institute, University of Chicago
(OIM 18175)

This macehead of diorite is pear-shaped and is perforated longitudinally.

70. Necklace

Diospolis Parva, Tomb U379
Clay and stone
Gerzean-Protodynastic
No measurements available
The Petrie Museum, University College London
(UC 10834-8)

The clay and stone beads surround two larger bucrania or bull head pendants of stone and ivory.

71. Bucrania or Bull Head Amulet

Hierakonpolis Main Deposit
Limestone
Gerzean-Protodynastic
Ht: 6.4 cm (2 1/2 in.)
The Petrie Museum, University College London
(UC 15002)

This circular stylized bull head has a flat base. A basal rim base and a short columnar neck join the back of the head. The amulet is perforated laterally at the back. The face of the amulet is flat with the two horns curving around the edge of the bottom half and up to the center, where the tips are slightly separated. Incised circles, with smaller circles in their centers, represent the eyes. The top of the head curves over to the back and converges with the neck. The polished buff-colored surface is cracked and soft in places. Recently, two similar pendants have been found in place in Gerzean-Protodynastic settlement-level excavations at Hierakonpolis.

72. Staff Handle(?)

Acquired in Egypt
Ivory or bone
Predynastic (Protodynastic?)
Lth: 5.4 cm x Diam. of end: 1.2 cm x Diam. of projection: 2.1 cm (2 1/8 in. x 1/2 in. x 5/8 in.)
Royal Ontario Museum, Toronto (910.92.10)

This tubular cylinder flares at both ends. In its center is a short circular bulge with a central hole to accommodate the now missing wooden (?) staff and two small lateral holes for the pins which would have secured the handle to the staff. Such an artifact was clearly a status symbol. Staffs were held by priests from Gerzean times through the Dynastic era.

73. Pot on Stand Model

Hierakonpolis Main Deposit
Faience
Protodynastic
Ht: 8.2 cm (3 1/4 in.)
The Petrie Museum, University College London
(UC 15011)

Faience model of a roll rim jar resting on a pot stand. The stand has rolled base and rim and triangular cut outs. Similar stands and jars have been found recently in the Protodynastic royal necropolis at Hierakonpolis. The surface is fairly smooth and off-white in color, with traces of a light green glaze.

71. Bucrania or Bull Head Amulet; Gerzean-Protodynastic; The Petrie Museum, University College London (UC 15002).

72. Staff Handle(?); Predynastic (Protodynastic?); Royal Ontario Museum, Toronto (910.92.10).

74. Dog Model; Protodynastic; The Petrie Museum, University College London (UC 11001).

74. Dog Model

Hierakonpolis Main Deposit
Clay
Protodynastic
Ht: 7.0 cm (2 3/4 in.)
The Petrie Museum, University College London
(UC 11001)

This faience model of a recumbent animal, probably a dog, has hind legs forming the flat base. The forelegs tilt slightly up from this base. Incised lines define the claws—two lines on back paws and three on front. A ridge from the back almost to the base represents the tail. The back curves up to the ears, the tips of which are broken off. The snout is pointed and the face slopes down from the ears. Two V-shaped lines are incised in front of the ears, which are incised ovals. The nostrils are two incised dots, and a ridge extends from them towards the eyes. A light green glaze outlines the mouth. Patches of white occur on the back, base and below the jaw.

75. Baboon Model

Hierakonpolis Main Deposit
Faience
Protodynastic
Ht: 5.2 cm (2 1/16 in.)
The Petrie Museum, University College London
(UC 11002)

Faience model of a baboon sits on a flat base. The legs are joined to the body in a kneeling position, indicated by raised, bent ridges. The tail is a ridge between the legs on the base. The back is straight and curved slightly to the neck. The forelimbs are ridges attached to the body and curved forward to the knees, with an object, probably a pot or a loaf, between them and the knees. This object has a pointed top and ends a little below the jaw. The head was once broken off at the neck and is now rejoined. A raised ridge indicates the snout. Rounded protuberances occur above the eye. An incised circle indicates one eye. Depressions form the ears. Most of the green glaze still remains, but it is chipped on one forelimb. A patch of off-white occurs on one side showing where the glaze has faded.

75. Baboon Model; Protodynastic; The Petrie Museum, University College London (UC 11002).

76. Scorpion Model; Protodynastic; The Petrie Museum, University College London (UC 11010).

76. Scorpion Model

Hierakonpolis Main Deposit
Pottery
Protodynastic
Ht: 6.2 cm (2 1/2 in.)
The Petrie Museum, University College London
(UC 11010)

This fairly crude model of a scorpion has an extended flattened peg projecting from the base, and a hole passes horizontally through the peg. It is possible that this piece was mounted on the end of a pole and carried as a standard. Clay is buff to pink. The scorpion's anterior is rounded, with no indication of the chelae. Pointed ridges

77. Female Statuette; Protodynastic; The Petrie Museum, University College London (UC 14860).

78. Rope-Shaped Beads; Protodynastic; The Petrie Museum, University College London (UC 14893).

80. Scorpion Model; Protodynastic; The Petrie Museum, University College London (UC 15021).

slope backward from the pedipalp attachment. Raised dots on top of the cephalothorax represent two eyes; these probably represent the median eyes. Lines incised on the top of the pre-abdomen separate seven segments. Three backward inverted, deeply incised V-shapes represent the legs along each side. The post-abdomen is broken off at the base and was probably crafted to show the scorpion ready to strike.

77. Female Statuette

Hierakonpolis Main Deposit
Ivory
Protodynastic
Ht: 20.0 cm (7 7/8 in.)
The Petrie Museum, University College London
(UC 14860)

Possibly carved from the hard center of the tip of an elephant tusk, this figure has a hole drilled in the top of the woman's head which may be a later alteration. A long rectangular wig at the back reaches below the waist and is decorated with horizontal incised lines imitating plaited or braided hair. Part of the wig protrudes below the large ears on each side of the neck to the shoulder. The broken nose makes the face appear flat. Incised lines form the eyebrows, eyes and mouth. The neck is short and the chest slopes to heavy pendulous breasts. Each arm is broken off at the shoulder. The right hand is in relief at the side of the upper thigh with incised fingers. The lower left arm is carved under the breasts. The right hand forms a fist with the thumb pointing up to the right breast. The center of the figure is marred by a deep crack which passes through the pudendum. An incised line separates the rounded buttocks and the legs. The lower part of the legs has been broken and mended. The feet form a rectangle with a central perforation. The back of the right heel is much lower than the foot and the crack between the heel and the foot may indicate that the front part of a peg is stuck on by mud in the wrong position. A peg on the base of the statuette indicates it was mounted on a base or on a staff at one time. The intact surface is smooth, vertically cracked, and a brown to buff color.

78. Rope-Shaped Beads

Hierakonpolis Main Deposit
Faience
Protodynastic
Average Lth: 4.0 to 5.0 cm (1 5/8 in. to 2 in.)
The Petrie Museum, University College London
(UC 14893)

These spiral-shaped beads total one hundred of the original find of 754 beads. The beads have a lengthwise circular hole. Some beads, representing rope ends, have one rounded tip; while other beads have two flattened ends. The surface varies from a poorly preserved powdery white without glaze to the original green-blue glaze. These beads may have been used for a door curtain and are designed to look like rope.

79. Statuette of Baboon and Offspring; Protodynastic; The Petrie Museum, University College London (UC 15000).

81. Palette; Late Protodynastic; The University Museum of The University of Pennsylvania (E-1240) (Neg. 138874).

83. Ape Amulet; Dynasty I (Archaic); The University Museum of The University of Pennsylvania (E-13373).

79. Statuette of Baboon and Offspring

Hierakonpolis Main Deposit
Limestone
Protodynastic
Ht: 10.3 cm (4 1/16 in.)
The Petrie Museum, University College London
(UC 15000)

The model, made from smoothed, buff-colored limestone with black patches, portrays a seated baboon holding its offspring between its paws. The adult's paws are shown as incised digits and the young baboon sits curled up holding paws with the adult. Its head is well carved and turned to face outwards. The baby's snout has nostrils; the eyes and the ears are carved. A broken patch occurs on the right side of the adult. The base of the statuette is flat. The tail curves along the base and up the left side of the hind limb. The adult's snout faces straight forward showing an incised mouth and nostrils pits. The raised brow ridges and eye circles are shown on each side of the head. The left eye is chipped.

80. Scorpion Model

Hierakonpolis Main Deposit
Limestone
Protodynastic
Ht: 7.3 cm (2 7/8 in.)
The Petrie Museum, University College London
(UC 15021)

The scorpion model sits on a flat base. The cephalothorax is separated from the abdomen by two curved channels on each side. The two front claws on the end of the cephalothorax have a raised triangle between them. No appendages appear on the pre-abdomen; but the tail, which is curved up from the flat base, has five. The tail sting is indicated as the shortest segment. The smooth surface is pink to buff.

81. Palette

Provenance unknown
Slate
Late Protodynastic
Diam: ll.0 cm (4 3/8 in.)
The University Museum, University of
Pennsylvania (E-1240)

The circular pigment palette is perforated for suspension.

82. Stela

Abydos, Umm el-Ga'ab, Tomb of King Djet
Limestone
Dynasty I (Archaic)
Ht: 23.7 cm x Wth: 16.7 cm (9 3/8 in. x 6 5/8 in.)
The University Museum, University of
Pennsylvania (E-9184)

This limestone stela (gravemarker) bears the name of a
valued retainer who was buried just outside the tomb of
King Djet. Some experts believe such servants were sacri-
ficed in the First Dynasty on the death of the king, but
definitive evidence is lacking.

83. Ape Amulet

Abydos
Earthenware with faience glaze
Dynasty I (Archaic)
Ht: 4.7 cm x Wth: 2.4 cm (1 7/8 in. x 15/16 in.)
The University Museum, University of
Pennsylvania (E-13373)

This green-glazed faience ape figurine has its forelimbs
extended with its legs forming the flat base. There are few
facial features other than the protruding snout. Surface
appears rough.

84. Stela

Abydos subsidiary grave III
Limestone
Dynasty I, time of Djer (Archaic)
Ht: 26.5 cm (10 1/2 in.)
The Petrie Museum, University College London
(UC 14271)

This stela has a carved portion of a retainer of King Djer.
The presence of this person's gravemarker at Abydos,
next to the royal tomb, indicates a position of some
importance. (see also 82)

85. Disk

Saqqara
Limestone
Dynasty I (Archaic)
Diam: 10.5 cm x Dth: 2.7 cm (4 1/4 in. x 7/8 in.)
Royal Ontario Museum, Toronto (909.80.44)

The disk, possibly a gaming piece, is flat on the bottom
surface and rises slightly towards the center upper surface. Animals that appear to be gazelles and a lion are
carved in low relief. Four perforations occur
assymetrically around the center perforation.

84. Stela; Dynasty I, time of Djer (Archaic); The Petrie Museum, University College London (UC 14271).

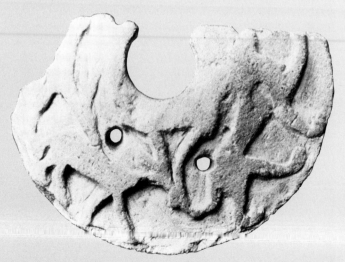

85. Disk; Dynasty I (Archaic); Royal Ontario Museum, Toronto
(909.80.44).

89

86. Offering Table; Dynasty II (Archaic); The Charleston Museum, South Carolina (ARM 237).

86. Offering Table

Sedment
Alabaster
Dynasty II (Archaic)
Ht: 9.9 cm x Diam: 33.5 cm (3 15/16 in. x 13 1/4 in.)
The Charleston Museum, South Carolina
(ARM 237)

This offering table is carved from white and grey patterned alabaster. Its polished circular top is supported by a deeply concave central pedestal. Offering tables were standard tomb equipment starting in Archaic times and were meant to hold offerings of food and drink for the spirit of the deceased.

87. Female Statuette

Provenance unknown
Limestone
Dynasty VI (Old Kingdom)
Ht: 10.1 cm (4 in.)
Harer Family Trust

Woman grinding grain. Statuettes like this were common in the later Old Kingdom and reflect that period's artistic interest in depicting everyday life.

88. Bas Relief of Five Figures

Provenance unknown
Stone
Dynasty XII (Middle Kingdom)
Ht: 17.8 cm x Wth: 39 cm (7 in. x 15 1/3 in.)
Harer Family Trust

Called a "Family group," these five figures face forward in upright positions. The base is inscribed with a single band of hieroglyphs, divided at the center yielding two *"htp di nyswt"* formula reading in opposite directions. In the spaces in between figures one, two, three, and four, appear three more "htp di nyswt" formulas, and figures one through four also bear inscriptions. *"Ka"* is the spirit or soul of an individual.

It translates:

An offering which king gives to Osiris, the great god, the lord of Abydos, for *"ka of Ibi,"* the vindicated, the possessor of an endowment. (or: the possessor of veneration) An offering which the king gives to *Wep-wa-wet,* the lord of Abydos, for the *ka* of *Ka-es...* (Ka-es is the other principle owner and is probably the wife of *Ibi)* An offering which the king gives to Osiris for the ka of the lady of the house, Ka-es..., the vindicated (Ka-es..., the vindicated appears on figure two, thus serving as a label for the figure, while the figure in turn serves as a determinative for the hieroglyphic inscription) An offering which the king gives to Wep-wa-wet for the ka of...*Hor-wer-nakht*, the vindicated. (name-Horus the elder is victorious) An offering which the king gives to Wep-wa-wet for the ka of the lady of the house...*Meri..?..*, the vindicated. (Translation by Gerry Scott, Peabody Museum of Natural History, New Haven.)

89. Male Statuette

Provenance unknown
Stone
Dynasty XII (Middle Kingdom)
Ht: 38.1 cm (15 in.)
Harer Family Trust

This seated male figure is of black igneous rock.

90. Bust Portion of Statuette

Provenance unknown
Stone
Dynasties XI-XII (Middle Kingdom)
Ht: 21.0 cm (8 1/4 in.)
Harer Family Trust

This front-facing female bust was once part of a complete figure which later broke at the waist.

91. House Model

Rifeh
Pottery
Dynasty XII (Middle Kingdom)
Ht: 30.5 cm x Wth: 40.7 cm (12 in. x 16 in.)
Gift of Egyptian Research Account
Museum of Fine Arts, Boston (07.551A)

This "soul house" was buried in a tomb to provide a home for the deceased's spirit. It is made from buff-colored clay and is rectangular in shape. The foreground is open and resembles a courtyard, while the back wall is solid with the exception of some cracking. There are two columns which support the low roof.

92. Priest Statuette

Hierakonpolis Temple
Serpentine
Dynasty XVIII (New Kingdom)
Ht: 18.0 cm (7 1/16 in.)
The Petrie Museum, University College London (UC 14880)

Only the upper part of a statuette carved of black to grey serpentine remains. The man's right side is broken below the shoulder and the body beneath the hips is missing.

91. House Model; Dynasty XII (Middle Kingdom); Gift of Egyptian Research Account; Museum of Fine Arts, Boston (07.551A).

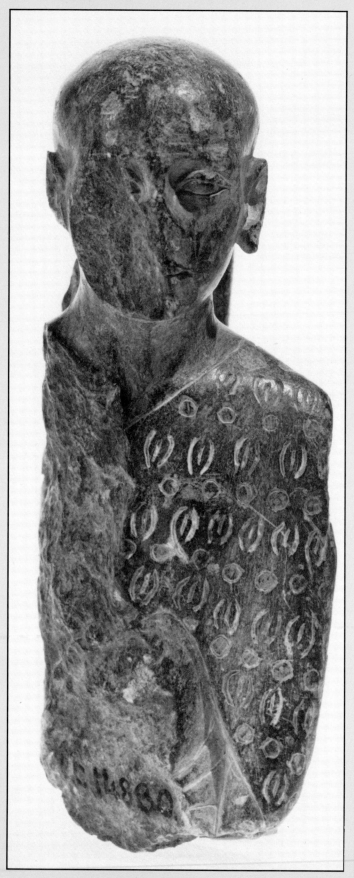

92. Priest Statuette; Dynasty XVIII (New Kingdom); The Petrie Museum, University College London (UC 14880).

95. Statuette of Neith; Dynasties XXVII-XXXII (Late Period or Early Ptolemaic); Royal Ontario Museum, Toronto (910.17.27).

The head is finely carved and both ears remain. The long lobes of the ears appear to be pierced. The left eye and the left side of the mouth are well carved. A patterned cloak, probably a leopard skin, is carved over the back, left shoulder and left arm, extending to the abdomen. Three lines beneath the abdomen on the left side indicate the top of a kilt. The possible remains of the right hand are below the end of the cloak at the abdomen. A back pillar displays a vertical incised inscription:

htp di Hr nhn(y) Hr nd it.f Hr nfr ntrw nb(w)

"A boon which the king gives to Horus of Nekhen, Harendotes and Horus the Beautiful, and all the gods."

93. Bas Relief of Pa Bas

Provenance unknown
Stone
Dynasties XVIII-XX (New Kingdom)
Ht: 33.6 cm x Wth: 33.6 cm (13 1/4 in. x 13 1/4 in.)
Harer Family Trust

This fragment of stone has the profile of an official thought to be Pa Bas.

94. Statuette

Provenance unknown
Bronze
Dynasty XXVI (Saite period)
Ht: 38.0 cm x Wth: 25.7cm (15 in. x 10 1/8 in.)
Florence Museum, South Carolina (933)

This cat figure sits on a flat base formed by its hind quarters. Forearms extend directly below the body. Tail wraps around from the back to the front legs. The head of the cat has eyes shown by indentations and incised circles. The face looks forward with ears extending upward from the head. The rounded back of the head extends down to the neck which gradually flows into the body. Surface has malachite patina, with some slight discoloration and wear. Major repairs have been made. Figurines like this are typical of the Saite Dynasty—a period which saw the last revival of art and political power under native Egyptian rulers.

95. Statuette of Neith

Provenance unknown
Bronze
Dynasties XXVII-XXXII (Late Period or Early Ptolemaic)
Ht. without tenon: 35.7 cm (14 in.)
Royal Ontario Museum, Toronto (910.17.27)

In this fine bronze statuette of the goddess Neith, both hands hold separately made sceptre and ankh, the cross of life. Only a portion of the ankh stem remains. Neith is dressed in a plain dress with a wide collar designed in relief around the neck. She wears no bracelets and the red crown she wears has a socket for a missing spiral. The

94. Statuette; Dynasty XXVI (Saite Period), Florence Museum, South Carolina (933).

97. Ushabti; Dynasties XXVII-XXXI (Late Period); The Charleston Museum, South Carolina (ARM 70).

94

98. Ceramic "Eye of Horus"; Dynasties XXVII-XXXI (Late Period); The Charleston Museum, South Carolina (ARM 70).

whites of the eyes were overlaid with gold, much of which is now missing. There are no traces of gold elsewhere. The solid cast object is of the highest quality and design. Tenons occur at two corners under the feet. The partially illegible inscription surrounds four sides of the base. Neith was a very ancient goddess whose distinctive harpoon or arrow symbols were already common in Predynastic times.

96. Ushabti

Probable Sedment
Wood
Dynasties XXVII-XXXI (Late Period)
Ht: 19.3 cm x Wth: 6.1 cm (7 5/8 in. x 2 3/8 in.)
The Charleston Museum, South Carolina (ARM 76)

Black, carved anthropoid figure has folded arms. It is apparently covered with pitch that has since worn off in places. The pitch probably comes from the mummy wrappings that hold the Ushabti or servant next to the body. There are traces of white paint. Ushabtis were placed in tombs to do work for their owner in the afterlife.

97. Ushabti

Probable Sedment
Wood
Dynasties XXVII-XXXI (Late Period)
Ht: 14.9 cm (5 7/8 in.)
The Charleston Museum, South Carolina (ARM 70)

This figure representing a tomb servant is a standing anthropoid figure with arms folded in a similar position to Ushabti (96) and has a turquoise faience glaze. The face has been broken off and there are hieroglyphs painted on the front of the lower body.

98. Ceramic "Eye of Horus"

Provenance unknown
Earthenware with faience
Dynasties XXVII-XXXI (Late Period)
Ht: 1.9 cm x Lth: 5.5 cm (7/8 in. x 2 1/4 in.)
The Charleston Museum, South Carolina
(ARM 196)

Left eye of Horus is made of earthenware with a blue faience glaze. The inner eye is black and white. The eye of Horus symbolizes the moon and was a common amulet in ancient Egypt.

99. Necklace with pendant

Provenance unknown
Ceramic
Probable Greco-Roman
Scarab-Ht: 9.1 cm x Wth: 0.95 cm (3 5/8 in. x 3/8 in.)
Beads-Lth: 0.8 cm to 1.2 cm (1/4 in. to 1/2 in.)
The Charleston Museum, South Carolina
(ARM 227)

A string of blue and turquoise faience glazed tubular beads are interspersed with flat and rounded discoidal beads. The three-piece pendant strung between the beads is made of blue faience and represents a winged scarab. The wings are attached to the body by strings through perforations. Some black paint appears on the dorsal side of the scarab and its wings. The scarab was a symbol of the sun god and rebirth.

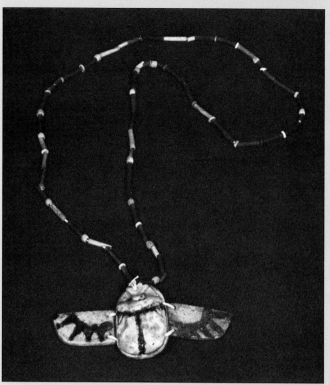

99. Necklace with Pendant; Probable Greco-Roman; The Charleston Museum, South Carolina (ARM 227).

100. Mummy Mask

Provenance unknown
Cartonage
Dynasty XXXII (Ptolemaic)
No measurements available
Harer Family Trust

Brilliantly colored mummy masks were typical of the Ptolemiac period and show the continuing popularity of ancient mortuary practices.

101. Linen Roll

Provenance unknown
Linen
Date undetermined
Lth: 12.0 cm x Wth: 6.0 cm (4 3/4 in. x 2 3/8 in.)
The Charleston Museum, South Carolina (ARM 116)

A roll of linen (*Linum* sp.) used in mummification. Linen was already being produced from flax in Predynastic times and was available in several qualities. It was commonly used for fine clothing as well as mummy wrappings.

101. Linen Roll; date undetermined; The Charleston Museum, South Carolina (ARM 116).

102. Acheulean Hand Axe; Late Lower Palaeolithic; Private Lender.

102. Acheulean Hand Axe

Gulf of Suez area
Flint
Late Lower Palaeolithic, ca. 300,000-120,000 B.C.
Ht: 18.0 cm x Wth: 10.5 cm x Cir: 23.0 cm (7 1/16 in. x 4 1/8 in. x 9 1/8 in.)
Private lender

This hand axe has been worked on two sides (bifacial). While there is no known direct association between Egyptian and European peoples, such hand tools are termed "Acheulean" after the site of St. Acheul in France where such implements were first scientifically described. Such implements were probably used for a variety of purposes by early man (*Homo erectus*), including digging, butchering and scraping hides. They are found in hunting and gathering camp sites all over the Sahara, indicating that the climate of the time was wetter than today and that the desert was probably a grassland.

This type of crude bifacial implement is common throughout Europe and Africa.

103. Worked Quartz Cobble

Gulf of Suez area
Quartz
Lower Palaeolithic
Ht: 8.0 cm x Wth: 4.0 cm x Cir: 13.0 cm (3 1/8 in. x 1 9/17 in. x 5 1/8 in.)
Private lender

This hand-sized stone or cobble has been shaped by crude percussion flaking. The quartz cobble may possibly have been used as a wood working tool. Tools like this have been dated back almost two million years at sites in East and South Africa.

104. Levallois Point; Middle Palaeolithic; The Charleston Museum, South Carolina (ARM 316).

108. Hollow Base Projectile Point; Neolithic; The Charleston Museum, South Carolina (ARM 308A).

104. Levallois Point

Found on the surface of the Theban Plateau
Flint
Middle Palaeolithic
No measurements available
The Charleston Museum, South Carolina (ARM 316)

This large brown Levallois flake point has a crude bifacial retouch along the two edges.

105. Knife

Gulf of Suez area
Flint
Early Neolithic
Ht: 9.5 cm x Wth: 4.0 cm (3 3/4 in. x 1 9/16 in.)
Private lender

Knife is bifacially pressure flaked and reflects increasing skill of Neolithic flint knappers.

106. Flake Scraper

Gulf of Suez area
Flint
Probable Neolithic
Ht: 8.0 cm x Wth: 5.5 cm (3 1/8 in. x 2 3/16 in.)
Private lender

This flake scraper has an alternate edge pressure retouch and part of the original cortex (weathered surface) of the parent rock is visible. Such scrapers were generally used to clean hides.

107. Hollow Base Projectile Point

Fayum
Flint
Neolithic
Ht: 4.4 cm x Wth: 2.8 cm (1 5/8 in. x 1 1/4 in.)
Private lender

Point shows fine pressure flaking and the diagnostic concave depression or "hollow" across its distal end. One tang is broken at the tip. Hollow base points are found in Northern Egyptian Neolithic sites like those in the Fayum and at Merimde and in most Upper Egyptian Predynastic localities; thus, they provide a useful means of cross-dating widely separated sites.

108. Hollow Base Projectile Point

Fayum
Flint
Neolithic
Ht: 4.8 cm x Wth: 2.8 cm (1 7/8 in. x 1 1/4 in.)
The Charleston Museum, South Carolina
(ARM 308A)

The point shows fine pressure flaking and has a hollow cresent-shaped base. (See 106) Such points are often carefully retouched.

109. Bifacial Sickle Blade

Fayum
Flint
Neolithic (probably Fayum A)
Ht: 5.5 cm x Wth: 2.4 cm (2 3/16 in. x 15/16 in.)
The Charleston Museum, South Carolina
(ARM 301A)

This bifacially retouched, serrated sickle blade midsection of tan flint is typical of the Fayum Neolithic (Fayum A). Originally, it was probably fixed onto a wooden or bone haft.

110. Bifacial Sickle Blade

Fayum
Flint
Neolithic (probably Fayum A)
Ht: 5.7 cm x Wth: 2.3 cm (2 1/4 in. x 1 1/8 in.)
The Charleston Museum, South Carolina (ARM 301B)

This bifacial retouched serrated sickle blade tip of tan flint was probably set in a wooden or bone haft.

111. Tanged Point

Fayum
Flint
Probable Neolithic/Predynastic
Lth: 4.7 cm x Wth: 1.2 cm x Dth: 0.3 cm (1 13/16 in. x 1 3/16 in. x 1/8 in.)
The Charleston Museum, South Carolina (ARM 309)

This tan tanged and barbed point is bifacially retouched.

112. Stemmed Microlithic Point

Fayum
Flint
Probable Neolithic/Predynastic
Lth: 3.1 cm x Wth: 1.9 cm x Dth: 0.3 cm (1 1/4 in. x 3/4 in. x 3/16 in.)
The Charleston Museum, South Carolina (ARM 311)

This tan microlith point has a contracting stem and exhibits bifacial retouch and was possibly used as an arrowhead, drill or engraver. Similar points have been excavated in Predynastic settlements.

113. Microlithic Point

Fayum
Flint
Probable Neolithic/Predynastic
Lth: 3.4 cm x Wth: 1.9 cm x Dth: 0.3 cm (1 3/8 in. x 3/8 in. x 1/8 in.)
The Charleston Museum, South Carolina (ARM 304)

This dark brown microlith point has fine bifacial retouch. Its blunt tip suggests its possible function as a punch or a drill.

109. Bifacial Sickle Blade; Neolithic; The Charleston Museum, South Carolina (ARM 301A).

110. Bifacial Sickle Blade; Neolithic; The Charleston Museum, South Carolina (ARM 301B).

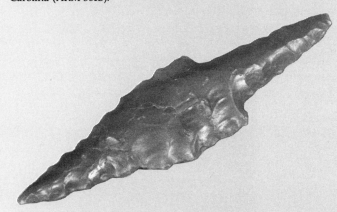

112. Stemmed Microlithic Point; Probable Neolithic/Predynastic; The Charleston Museum, South Carolina (ARM 311).

113. Microlithic Point; Probable Neolithic/Predynastic; The Charleston Museum, South Carolina (ARM 304).

114. Harpoon; Predynastic; Harvard University/Museum of Fine Arts Expedition; Museum of Fine Arts, Boston (11.295).

115. Copper Needle; Amratian-Gerzean (Naqada I-early Naqada II); Kom el-Ahmar, H. de Morgan's excavations, 1907-1908; 17.0 cm; The Brooklyn Museum,(09.889.294A) Museum Collection Fund.

114. Harpoon

Mesaeed
Copper
Predynastic
No measurements available
Harvard University/Museum of Fine Arts
Expedition
Museum of Fine Arts, Boston (11.295)

Harpoons such as this were used for fishing on the Nile. Copper was a rare commodity in Predynastic times and was often melted down for re-use. The preservation of a copper Predynastic tool is rare.

115. Needle

Kom el Ahmar (Kom el Ahmar no. 92),
Hierakonpolis
H. de Morgan's excavation, 1907-1908
Copper
Amratian-Gerzean
Ht: 2.8 cm x Diam: 11.0 cm (1 1/8 in. x 4 3/8 in.)
The Brooklyn Museum, (09.889.294a)

This needle is long, thin and curved. The hole of the needle is formed from bending back the end.

116. Fish-Tail Biface

Abydos
Flint
Amratian-Gerzean
Lth: 14.0 cm x Wth: 7.6 cm (4 5/8 in. x 2 1/8 in.)
Royal Ontario Museum, Toronto (910x56.65)

This flint artifact is bifacially flaked and unusually thick. It has shallow concave base and irregular pressure flaking on the surface. One lower lateral margin is crude and battered. White cortex appears on butt and lower face. This object has also been called a "lancehead;" but, actu-

117. Fish-Tail Biface; Amratian-Gerzean; Royal Ontario Museum, Toronto (910x55.5).

116. Fish-Tail Biface; Amratian-Gerzean; Royal Ontario Museum, Toronto (910x56.65).

ally, it was mounted with the concave end outward. It is believed to have been used in rituals or ceremonies connected with the mortuary cult.

117. Fish-Tail Biface

Abydos
Flint
Amratian-Gerzean
Lth: 11.8 cm x Wth: 2.3 cm (4 5/8 in. x 7/8 in.)
Royal Ontario Museum, Toronto (910x55.5)

The grey-rose flint fish-tail is bifacial and has fine denticulation on the edges of one end which continue laterally for about 5.0 cm. The tool thickens towards the point. The edges are thin and sharp.

118. Ripple Flaked Knife

Abu Zaidan (Abu Zaidan no. 102)
Flint
Late Gerzean (Late Naqada II)
Lth: 28.8 cm (11 3/8 in.)
The Brooklyn Museum, (09.889.119)
Museum Collection Fund

The knife is intact with the exception of a large chip in the cutting edge.

119. Ripple Flaked Knife

Egypt
Flint
Late Gerzean-Protodynastic
Lth: 24.6 cm (9 11/16 in.)
The Oriental Institute, University of Chicago
(OIM 9390)

The knife is crescent-shaped with fine ripple flaking on one face and a smooth ground surface on the opposite side. The edge is finely serrated. The knife has been broken and repaired. Knives like these were often mounted in decorated handles of ivory or gold and buried with rich and powerful individuals. They represent a high point in the flint making craft and were produced by specialists.

120. Ripple Flaked Knife

Abydos
Flint
Late Gerzean-Protodynastic
Lth: 24.3 cm x Wth: 6.0 cm (9 5/8 in. x 2 3/8 in.)
Royal Ontario Museum, Toronto (986x2.31)

One side of the mottled yellowish-brown flint knife has been extensively worked with fine retouching. The other side is ground smooth with some retouching at the butt end and along the top edge. The lower edge is finely serrated to within 3 inches of the butt end. The blade has been broken and repaired.

118. Ripple Flaked Knife; Late Gerzean (Late Naqada II); Abu Zaidan (Abu Zaidan no. 102); Lth: 28.8 cm; The Brooklyn Museum, (09.889.119) Museum Collection Fund.

120. Ripple Flaked Knife; Late Gerzean-Protodynastic; Royal Ontario Museum, Toronto (986x2.31).

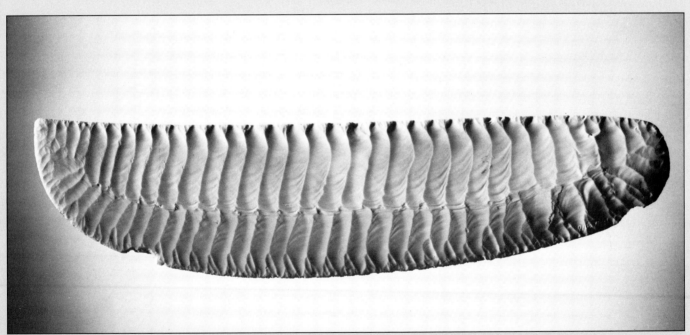

121. Ripple Flaked Knife; Protodynastic; Royal Ontario Museum, Toronto (910.55.1).

124. Axe Head from Tomb of Khasekhemui; Dynasty II (Archaic) ca. 2750 B.C.; The University Museum of The University of Pennsylvania (E-9577) (Neg. 138877).

121. Ripple Flaked Knife

Abydos area
Flint
Protodynastic
Lth: 24.6 cm x Wth: 5.7 cm (9 3/4 in. x 2 1/4 in.)
Royal Ontario Museum, Toronto (910.55.1)

This is a rose-buff flint knife ripple flaked similar to one described in 120.

122. Arrow Point from the Tomb of Djer

Abydos
Ivory
Dynasty I (Archaic)
Ht: 8.2 cm (3 1/4 in.)
The University Museum, University of
Pennsylvania (E-9409)

A long, thin point found in tomb of Djer. Such points would have topped reed arrow shafts and may have been dipped in poison before use.

123. Knife Impressed with Horus Banner and Hieroglyphs of Djer

Purchased in Luxor
Flint and gold
Dynasty I (Archaic)
Lth: 36.9 cm x Wth: 8.9 cm x Wth. at handle: 3.1 cm x Lth. of handle: 7.5 cm (14 1/2 in. x 3 1/2 in. x 1 1/4 in. x 3 in.)
Royal Ontario Museum, Toronto (914.3)

The Horus name of King Djer is inscribed on the gold foil wrapped over the handle of this flint knife. The knife is thin and crescent shaped and the handle is flaked to imitate the tangs of metal (copper) implements. The knife has been carefully produced by controlling pressure flaking and the cutting edge retouched by removing very small flakes. The shape and technique of manufacture are typical of the Archaic period and, though impressive, do not achieve the standards of earlier (late Gerzean-Protodynastic) ripple flaked knives. Although the royal inscription on this object indicates that it either belonged to King Djer or was a special gift given by the ruler, similar versions of such large flint knives were used in everyday tasks such as butchering and have been found in the Archaic town at Hierakonpolis.

124. Axe Head from Tomb of Khasekhemui

Abydos
Copper
Dynasty II (Archaic) ca. 2750 B.C.
Ht: 9.4 cm (3 3/4 in.)
The University Museum, University of
Pennsylvania (E 9577)

This small axe head is of beaten copper. Found in the Tomb of King Khasekhemui at Abydos, it is an example of

125. Adze; Dynasties III-VI (Early Dynastic-Old Kingdom); The Brooklyn Museum, (07.447.4) Museum Collection Fund.

126. Axe; Probable Dynasty XII (Middle Kingdom); Royal Ontario Museum, Toronto (909.80.218).

miniature tools and decorative items buried with the deceased for use in the afterlife.

125. Adze

From el'Adaima, H. de Morgan's excavations, 1906-07
Copper
Dynasties III-VI (Early Dynastic-Old Kingdom)
Lth: 17.0 cm (6 3/4 in.)
The Brooklyn Museum, (07.447.4)
Museum Collection Fund

This copper adze was reportedly found in an intact jar in a settlement.

126. Axe

Provenance unknown, purchased in Egypt
Copper
Probable Dynasty XII (Middle Kingdom)
Lth: 36.9 cm x Wth: 59.4 cm (14 1/2 in. x 2 3/4 in.)
Royal Ontario Museum, Toronto (909.80.218)

The scalloped copper axe has a shallow blade with small turned down lugs. There are five perforations at each end and four in the center for attachment to a shaft. A low flange surrounds the scallops. The axe is well preserved except for a small chip in blade.

127. Tweezers

Hu, Grave Y 501
Bronze
Dynasty XIII (Second Intermediate Period)
Lth: 7.5 cm x Wth. of the blade: 1.5 cm (2 5/16 in. x 3/16 in.)
The Oriental Institute, University of Chicago (OIM 5352)

These bronze tweezers have a round band and flattened triangular ends.

127. Tweezers; Dynasty XIII (Second Intermediate Period); Courtesy of The Oriental Institute of The University of Chicago (OIM 5352) (P.67641/ N.46417).

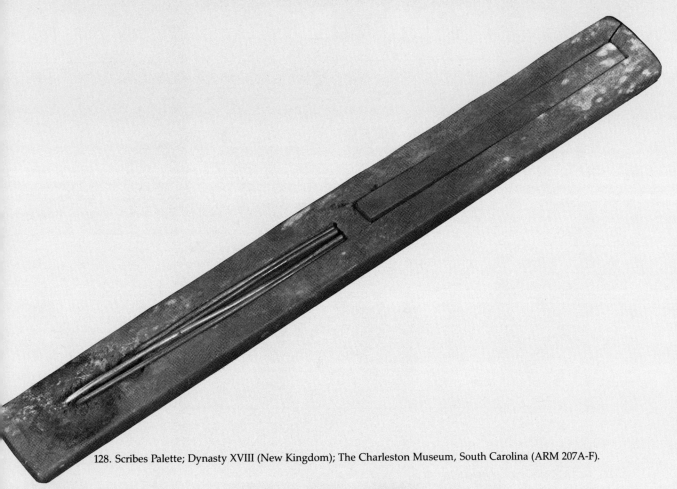

128. Scribes Palette; Dynasty XVIII (New Kingdom); The Charleston Museum, South Carolina (ARM 207A-F).

128. Scribe's Writing Palette

Ghurob
Wood and reeds
Dynasty XVIII (New Kingdom)
Lth: 36.2 cm x Wth: 4.27 cm (14 1/4 in. x 1 7/8 in.)
The Charleston Museum, South Carolina
(ARM 207A-F)

This brown, wooden writing palette has four reeds located within the reed compartment. Two holes are carved into the top surface for paints. Traces of black and red paint remain. The palette is cracked at one end and at the crosspieces above the opening to the reed compartment. Traces of paint are present on both ends of all the reeds.

129. Slate Palette

Medinet Habu
Slate
Dynasty XXII (Third Intermediate Period)
Lth: 8.0 cm x Wth: 5.7 cm x Dth: 0.9 cm (3 1/16 in. x 2 1/4 in. x 3/8 in.)
The Oriental Institute, University of Chicago
(OIM 14503)

This rectangular slate palette is slightly convex both front and back. It was probably used for writing. One side is decorated with two incised lines running around the edge.

Addendum

In addition to the artifacts catalogued, "The First Egyptians" exhibited the following:

Cast of the Narmer Palette:
Full size, and authentically colored. Lent by the Petrie Museum, University College London.

Cast of boat petroglyph at Hierakonpolis, (locality 61);
Cast of giraffe petroglyph at Hierakonpolis, (locality 61):
Both full size, authentically colored and prepared from latex molds taken at the site by Pat Hill Cresson.

Idealized stratifigraphic cross-section of Nehken showing definitive pottery changes through Predynastic to Dynastic time (Ht: 4 ft. x Wth: 4 ft. x Dth: 4 in.); First Dynasty Palace model (Lth: 4 ft. x Wth: 4 ft. x Ht: 7 in.): Both prepared by Jano Bell Fairservis, Sharon, Connecticut.

Amratian house and kiln model (Ht: 4 5/8 in. x Wth: 25 1/2 in. x Dth: 25 1/2 in.); Gerzean temple complex model (Ht: 15 in. x Wth: 54 in. x Dth: 44 in.): Both prepared by Roger Pelletier, Washington, D.C.

EVOLUTION OF POT FORMS

Amratian

Gerzean

Protodynastic

108

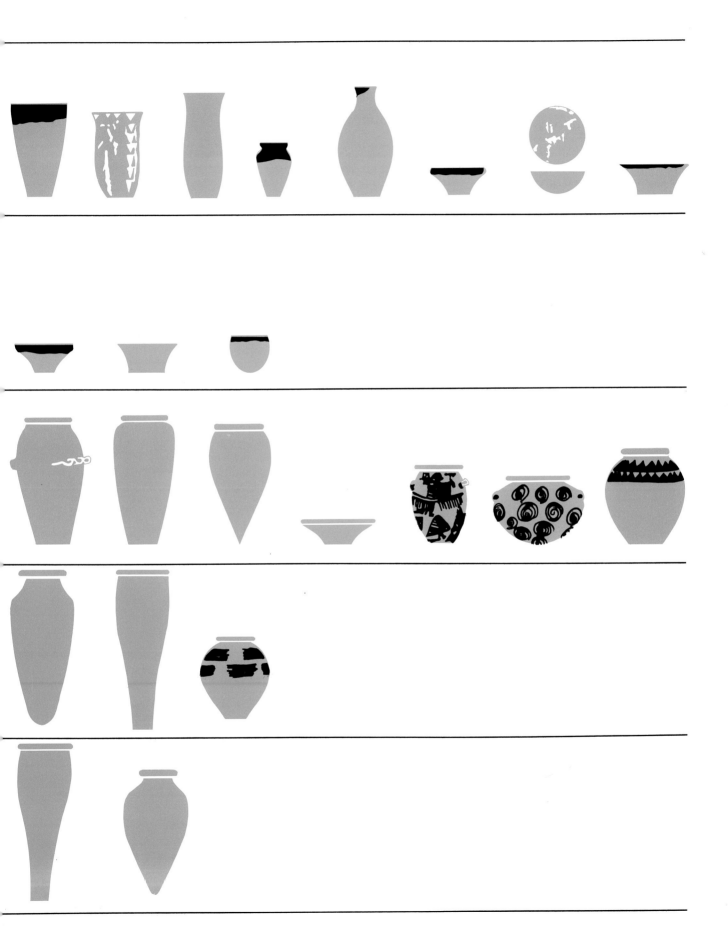

SELECTED BIBLIOGRAPHY

Adams, B., 1987, *The Fort Cemetery at Hierakonpolis Excavated by John Garstang*, London.

1974-, *Ancient Hierakonpolis (and Supplement)*. Aris and Phillips, Ltd., Warminster, England.

Adams, W. Y., 1977, *Nubia: Corridor to Africa*. Princeton University Press, Princeton, New Jersey.

Aldred, C., 1965, *Egypt to the End of the Old Kingdom*. Thames and Hudson, London.

Allen, R. O. & Hamroush, H., 1986, "Prehistoric Ceramic Technology," *Chemtech*, 16(8), pp. 484-8.

Allen, R. O. & Rogers, M. S., 1982 "A Geochemical Approach to the Understanding of Ceramic Technology in Ancient Egypt," *Archaeometry*, 24, 2, pp. 199-212.

Amelineau, E., 1899, *Les nouvelles fouilles d'Abydos, 1, 1885-1896*. Ed. Leroux, Paris.

Amiran, R. & Glass, J., 1979, "An Archaeological-Petrographical Study of 15 W-ware pots in the Ashmolean Museum," *Tel Aviv*, 6, 1-2.

Arnett, W.S., 1982, *The Predynastic Origin of Egyptian Hieroglyphs*, Washington.

Baumgartel, E.J., 1955, 1960, *The Cultures of Prehistoric Egypt*, Vol. I & II, London.

Boreux, C., 1908, "Les Poteries decorees de l'Egypte Predynastique," *Revue des Etudes Ethnographiques et Sociologiques*, pp. 1-20.

Bourriau, J., 1984, *Umm el Ga'ab: Pottery from the Nile Valley before the Arab Conquest*, Cambridge.

Brunton, G., 1932, "The Predynastic Town-site Hierakonpolis," in *Studies Presented to F. Ll. Griffiths*, London: 272-276.

Brunton, G. & Caton-Thompson, G., 1928, *The Badarian Civilization and Predynastic Remains near Badari*, British School of Archaeology in Egypt, London.

1975- , passim, *Bulletin de Liason du Groupe International pour l'Etude de la Ceramique Egyptienne*, Cairo.

Butzer, K.W., 1976, *Early Hydraulic Civilization in Egypt: A Study in Cultural Ecology*. University of Chicago Press, Chicago.

1974- , "Modern Egyptian Pottery Clays and Predynastic Buff Ware," *Journal of Near Eastern Studies*, 33, pp.377-382.

Capart, J., 1905, *Primitive Art in Egypt*, London.

Caton-Thompson, G., 1934, *The Desert Fayum*. Royal Anthropological Institute, London.

Caton-Thompson, G. & Whittle, E., 1975, "Thermoluminescence Dating of the Badarian," *Antiquity*, 49, pp.89-97.

Derricourt, R. M., 1971, "Radiocarbon Chronology for Egypt and North Africa," *JNES*, 30:271-292.

Edwards, I. E. S., 1972, *The Pyramids of Egypt*, 3rd ed. Viking Press, New York.

Emery, W. B., 1961, *Archaic Egypt*. Harmondsworth, England.

Fairservis, W.A., 1986, *Hierakonpolis Project*. Vassar College, Poughkeepsie, New York.

1983- , *Hierakonpolis - The Graffiti and the Origins of Egyptian Hieroglyphic Writing*, Occasional Papers no. II, Poughkeepsie.

1972- , "Preliminary Report on the First Two Seasons at Hierakonpolis," *JARCE*, 9:7-27, 67-99.

1962- , *The Ancient Kingdoms of the Nile*. A Mentor Book, New York.

Finkenstaedt, E., 1981, "The Location of Styles in Painting: White Cross-Lined Ware at Naqada," *Journal of the American Research Center in Egypt*, XVIII, pp.7-10.

Frankfort, H., 1951, *The Birth of Civilization in the Near East*. Indiana University Press, Bloomington, Indiana.

Gardiner, A. H., 1961, *Egypt of the Pharaohs*. Oxford University Press, London.

1935- , *The Attitude of the Ancient Egyptians to Death and the Dead*. Cambridge University Press, Cambridge.

Garstang, J., 1907, "Excavations at Hierakonpolis, at Esna and in Nubia," *ASAE*, VII:132-148.

Geller, J.R., 1984, *The Predynastic Ceramics Industry at Hierakonpolis*, M.A. Thesis, St. Louis.

Hayes, W.C., 1965, *Most Ancient Egypt* (ed. by Keith Seele). University of Chicago Press, Chicago.

Hoffman, M.A., 1980, *Egypt Before the Pharaohs*. Routledge & Kegan Paul Ltd., London.

1976- , "City of the Hawk—Seat of Egypt's Ancient Civilization," *Expedition*, 18:32-41.

1974- , "The Social Context of Trash Disposal in the Early Dynastic Egyptian Town," *American Antiquity*, 39:35-50.

1972a- , "Occupational Features at the Kom el Ahmar," *JARCE*, 9:35-47.

1972b- , "Excavations at Locality 14," *JARCE*, 9:49-74.

1970- , *Culture History and Cultural Ecology at Hierakonpolis from Palaeolithic Times to the Old Kingdom*. Doctoral dissertation, University of Wisconsin, Madison.

Hoffman, M.A. et.al., 1982, *The Predynastic of Hierakonpolis*, Egyptian Studies Association Publication no.1, Cairo & Illinois.

Hope, C.A., 1987, *Egyptian Pottery*, Aylesbury.

Huzayyin, S.A., 1941, *The Place of Egypt in Prehistory: A Correlated Study of Climate and Cultures in the Old World*. MIE, Vol. XLIII, Cairo.

Kaiser, W., 1956, "Zur Inneren Chronologie de Naqadakultur," *Archaeologia Geographica*, 6, pp.69-77.

Kantor, H., 1965, "The Relative Chronology of Egypt and its Foreign Correlations before the Late Bronze Age," Ehrich, R.W., ed., *Chronologies in Old World Archaeology*, Chicago, pp.1-46.

Kemp, B.J., 1982, "Automatic Analysis of Predynastic Cemeteries: A New Method for an Old Problem," *Journal of Egyptian Archaeology*, 68, pp.5-15.

1972- , "Temple and Town in Ancient Egypt," in *Man, Settlement and Urbanism*, ed. by Ucko, Tringham, and Dimbleby, Duckworth, London: 657-680.

1966- , "Abydos and the Royal Tombs of the First Dynasty," *JEA*, 52:13-22.

Kroeper, K. & Wildung, D., 1985, *Minshat Abu Omar*, Munchner Ostdelta Expedition, SAS, Heft 3.

Lansing, A., 1935, "The Egyptian Expedition (at Hierakonpolis) 1934-1935," *Bulletin of the Metropolitan Museum of Art*, section II, November:37-45.

Lauer, J.-P., 1976, *Saqqara, The Royal Cemetery of Memphis*. Thames and Hudson, London.

Lucas, A., and J. R. Harris, 1962, *Ancient Egyptian Materials and Industries*, 4th ed. E. Arnold, London.

Massoulard, E., 1949, *Prehistoire et protohistoire de l'Egypte*. Travaux et memoires de l'Institut d'ethnologie, Universite de Paril, LIII, Paris.

McHugh, W.P., 1974, "Late Prehistoric Cultural Adaptation in Southwest Egypt and the Problem of the Nilotic Origins of Saharan Cattle Pastoralism," *JARCE*, XI:2-29.

Mond, R. & Myers, O., 1940, *Cemeteries of Armant, I*, Egypt Exploration Society, London.

de Morgan, J., 1897, *Recherches sur les origines de l'Egypte, II*. Leroux, Paris.

1896- , *Recherches sur les origines de l'Egypte, I*. Leroux, Paris.

Murray, M.A., 1920, "The First Mace-head of Hierakonpolis," *Ancient Egypt*, 15-17.

Needler, W., 1984, *Predynastic and Archaic Egypt in the Brooklyn Museum*, New York.

Nordstrom, H-A., 1972, *Neolithic and A-Group Sites*, 2 vols, Lund.

O'Connor, David, 1972, "The Geography of Settlement in Ancient Egypt," in *Man, Settlement and Urbanism*, ed. by Ucko, Tringham, and Dimbleby, Duckworth, London: 681-698.

Oren, E., 1973, "The Overland Route between Egypt and Canaan in the Early Bronze Age," *Israel Exploration Journal*, 23, pp.198-205.

Payne, J. Crowfoot, forthcoming, "Prehistory B: From Naqada I to the end of the Archaic Period," *Introduction to Ancient Egyptian Pottery*, Cairo.

Payne, J. Crowfoot, Kaczmarczyk, A. and Fleming, S.J., 1977, "Forged Decoration on Predynastic Pots," *Journal of Egyptian Archaeology, 63*, pp.5-12.

Peet, T.E., 1914, *The Cemeteries of Abydos, Part II, 1911-1912*. EES, 34, London.

Peet, T.E. and W. L. S. Loat, 1913, *The Cemeteries of Abydos, Part III, 1912-1913*. EES, 35, London.

4. Necked Vase; Amratian; Royal Ontario Museum, Toronto (910.85.88).

Petrie, W.M.F., 1953, *Ceremonial Slate Palettes and Corpus of Protodynastic Pottery*. B.S.A.E., London.

1932- , *Seventy Years in Archaeology*. H. Holt & Co., New York.

1921- , *Corpus of Prehistoric Pottery and Palettes*, B.S.A.E., London.

1920- , *Prehistoric Egypt*. British School of Archaeology and Egyptian Research Account, Publ. no. 31, London.

1903- , *Abydos, Part II, 1903*. Kegan Paul, Trench Trubner and Co., EES, 24, London.

1902- , *Abydos, Part I, 1902*. Kegan Paul, Trench, Trubner and Co., EES, 22, London.

1901- , *The Royal Tombs of the First Dynasty, Part II*. Kegan Paul, Trench, Trubner and Co., London.

1900- , *The Royal Tombs of the First Dynasty, Part I*. Kegan Paul, Trench, Trubner and Co., London.

Petrie, W.M.F., and A.C. Mace, 1901, *Diospolis Parva: The Cemeteries of Abadiyeh and Hu, 1898-1899*. Kegan Paul, Trench, Trubner and Co., EES, XX, London.

Petrie, W.M.F. & Quibell, J.E., 1896, *Naqada and Ballas 1895*, Egyptian Research Account, London.

Pfeiffer, J., 1976, *The Emergence of Society*. Harper & Row, New York.

Porat, N., 1987, "Trade of Pottery between Egypt and Canaan in Ancient Times," *Israeli Academic Center in Cairo Newsletter*, issue no.8.

Quibell, J.E., 1900, *Hierakonpolis I*. ERA, IV, London.

Quibell, J.E., and F.W. Green, 1902, *Hierakonpolis II*. ERA, V, London.

Randall-Maciver, D., and A.C. Mace, 1902, *El Amrah and Abydos, 1899-1901*. EES, XXIII, London.

Reisner, G.A., 1936, *The Development of the Egyptian Tomb Down to the Accession of Cheops*. Harvard University Press, Cambridge, Massachusetts.

Rizkana, I. & Seeher, J., 1984, "New Light on the Relation of Maadi to the Upper Egyptian Cultural Sequence," *Mitteilungen des Deutschen Archaologischen Institut Abteilung Kairo*, 40, pp.237-252.

Saad, Z.Y., 1969, *The Excavations at Helwan: Art and Civilization in the First and Second Egyptian Dynasties*. University of Oklahoma Press, Norman, Oklahoma.

Said, R., 1975, "The Geological Evolution of the River Nile," in *Problems in Prehistory: North Africa and the Levant*, ed. by Fred Wendorf and Anthony Marks, SMU Press, Dallas:7-44.

1962- , *The Geology of Egypt*. Elsevier Publ., Amsterdam and New York.

Smith, H.S., 1972, "Society and Settlement in Ancient Egypt," in *Man, Settlement and Urbanism*, ed. by Ucko, Tringham, and Dimbleby, Duckworth, London:705-720.

Smith, W.S., 1958, *The Art and Architecture of Ancient Egypt*. Penguin Books, Harmondsworth, England.

Trigger, B.G., 1976, *Nubia Under the Pharaohs*. Westview Press, Boulder, Colorado.

Vandier, J., 1952, *Manuel d'Archeologie Egyptienne I: les epoques de formation*, Paris.

Wendorf, F., and R. Said, 1976, *Prehistory of the Nile Valley*. Academic Press, New York.

Wilson, J.A., 1955, "Buto and Hierakonpolis in the Geography of Egypt," *JNES*, XIV:209-236.

1951- , *The Burden of Egypt* (republished as *The Culture of Ancient Egypt*). University of Chicago Press, Chicago.

Winkler, H.A., 1939, *Rock-Drawings of Southern Upper Egypt, II*. EES, London.

1938- , *Rock-Drawings of Southern Upper Egypt, I*. EES, London.

2. Bowl; Probable Amratian; The Charleston Museum, South Carolina (ARM 11).

T he First Egyptians" has required the concerted efforts of many individuals from the planning stage to the final production. The concept of the exhibition came through the conversations of Michael A. Hoffman, George D. Terry and Karin L. Willoughby. The magnitude of the exhibition increased as the discussions evolved and what was to be a small exhibition of artifacts collected by the University of South Carolina's Hierakonpolis expedition became the most comprehensive overview of the Predynastic people of Egypt to date.

It is almost impossible to thank each individual who has worked to make this presentation a reality. However, McKissick Museum is particularly grateful to the Earth Sciences and Resources Institute and the Hierakonpolis expedition of the University of South Carolina for their partnership in this project. The efforts of both organizations provided the research and the guiding philosophy which made the exhibition possible.

5. Vase; Amratian; (c) 1987 The Detroit Institute of Arts (79.44.1); Founders Society Purchase, Acquisitions Fund.

ACKNOWLEDGEMENTS

The staff of the exhibition would like to thank the many people too numerous to mention who have assisted with this exhibition.

Karin L. Willoughby, Curator of Natural Sciences at McKissick Museum and Exhibition Curator, directed her energies to the challenge of making the concepts a reality. She tackled the job of bringing both didactic and aesthetic elements to the presentation as well as consistency and clarity to the final product.

Dr. George D. Terry, Director of McKissick Museum, coordinated the activities between the University administration, the Earth Sciences and Resources Institute and the Museum. His efforts aroused the interest of the University, community and museums nationwide.

Elizabeth B. Stanton, Project Coordinator and Exhibition Registrar, performed many duties during the planning and implementation stages of the exhibition including dealing with the lending and host institutions concerning the objects in the exhibition and writing the catalog descriptions and index.

Lynn Robertson Myers, Chief Curator at McKissick, provided invaluable help in coordinating the catalog. Her advice was also helpful throughout the planning and design of the exhibition.

A special acknowledgement is due to the President of the University, James B. Holderman, as well as to Kenneth Schwab and Chris Vlahoplus. Their constant support of this project as well as other programs has been a significant part of the Museum's success.

Dr. Michael A. Hoffman, Director of the Expedition, Project Director of the Exhibition and Guest Curator, coordinated the research, both past and present, needed for the exhibition. His guidance and support ensured the success of the exhibition.

The efforts of a considerable number of individuals made the writing of the original grant to the National Endowment for the Humanities possible. Majken Blackwell, Larry Cameron, Pat H. Cresson, Jan B. Fairservis, Walter Fairservis, Renee Friedman, Susan Gawarecki, Fekri A. Hassan, Zahi Hawass, Craig Kridel, Peggy Nunn, David O'Connor, Roger Pellietier, Curtiss Peterson, Constance M. Prynne, Barbara Seagraves, Lynda Smith and

Barbara Tartaglia offered their technical and professional support.

A substantial debt is owed to the staff of the Earth Sciences and Resources Institute. The aid of many individuals made this exhibition possible, including: Dr. William H. Kanes, Mari A. Custodio, Elizabeth H. Morris, Cynthia Heaton, Jay Mills, Ricardo Pantonial and Catherine Smith.

Grateful appreciation is due Barbara Adams, not only for her informative essay on Egyptian Predynastic pottery, but for her service as a consultant through various phases of the project. Her cooperation in selecting objects from her collection for the exhibition is also very much appreciated. The objects from the Petrie Collection represent some of the finest examples of Predynastic artifacts and their presence would have been impossible without Mrs. Adams' assistance.

A special note of gratitude must be extended to special staff members at the institutions who lent objects and will travel the exhibition. Ginny Beaty, Edward Brovarski, Richard A. Fazzini, Jan Hiester, the Harer Family Trust, Marsha Hill, Peter Lacovara, Heather Maximea, Cara McEarchern, William H. Peck, Allyson H. Remz, Raymond D. Tindel and Martha Zierden were invaluable in the attainment of objects for loan. Carter Lupton, Peter Keller, Sheila Mutchler and Barbara Stone assisted in providing locations to which "The First Egyptians" will travel.

The staff at McKissick Museum assisted daily to the advance of the project. In particular, assistant curators Rachel Cockrell and Karen Klein were invaluable throughout the planning and implementation of the project. They filled many capacities and worked many long hours. Appreciation is also due to Maria Ballard, Gordon Brown, Vanessa Brown, John Heiting, Dale Kostelny, Peggy Nunn, Ann Salter, Mark Smith and Vincent Suttles. Excellent additional editing was provided by Arthur B. Leible and Ralph H. Willoughby.

The visual integrity of the exhibition was the key responsibility of Tom Kinnard. He devised the environment in which the objects were to be displayed. His concepts were given reality through the efforts of Majken Blackwell, coordinator of graphics and Alice Bouknight, coordinator of the installation staff.

A special thank you is also due to Lynn Eldridge and Lewis Zeigler of the Instructional Service Center for overseeing the production of the video components for "The First Egyptians." Their efforts were enhanced by the scriptwriter John Lucas.

The final visual presentation of the exhibition would not have been possible without the hard work of many people within the University. David Rinker, in particular, provided valuable support and guidance. The publications associated with "The First Egyptians" would have been an impossible task were it not for the aid of the Publications and Graphics units of the Division of University Relations at the University of South Carolina who provided concept, design and supervised production of print materials.

In recognition of their photographic contributions, we would like to thank Dirk Bakker, The Detroit Institute of Arts; John Lawson, The Oriental Institute, University of Chicago; Terry Richardson, The Charleston Museum, South Carolina; and Bill Robertson, Royal Ontario Museum, Toronto.

Finally this project would not have been at all possible if it had not been for the major funding provided by the National Endowment for the Humanities.

GLOSSARY

Abydos - The supposed site of the tomb of Osiris is located in this Middle Egyptian city. Many pilgrimages were made to the site in the hopes of eternal life. In the twentieth century, Archaic royal tombs were discovered and excavated.

Adze - A cutting tool that has a thin arched blade set at right angles to the handle. It was chiefly used for shaping wood.

Amratian Period - (ca. 3800-3500/3400 B.C.) Named after el Amrah site, this period is characterized by a fancy white cross-lined on polished red ware, black-topped red burnished pottery, stone vases and small, diamond-shaped slate palettes.

Black Land - The term refers to the fertile Nile Valley. It is translated from the Egyptian word *"kemet."*

Badarian Period - (ca. 5500/4000-3800 B.C.) Named for the site, el Badari, this period is characterized by three main types of fancy ware: polished red, polished black and black-topped polished red or brown pottery.

Bifacial - Two sides or faces of knife or point are finished.

Black-topped red ware - (black-topped Plum-Ware or B-class). Hand-made pottery that has a polished red surface and a blackened area below the rim. The vessel is placed upside down in dung, which causes oxidation reduction and produces the black color.

Breccia - Sedimentary rock comprised of angular fragments.

Burnishing - The technique of polishing leather-hard clay to a smooth finish.

Cartonage - Layers of linen glued together with a gesso surface.

Cephalothorax - The uniting of the head and thorax (breastplate) of an arachnid or higher crustacean.

Chalcolithic - The Copper Age.

Cross-dating - An object or group of objects are compared to similar pieces found in dateable contexts at other sites to estimate the age of the artifact.

Decorated (D-class) - Smooth surface pottery with designs in an ocher wash (red iron oxide) of plum-red hue. Named by Petrie.

Diorite - Often used by Egyptians in their sculpture, diorite is an extremely hard igneous rock of salt and pepper color.

Djer - A king of the First Dynasty.

Djet - A king of the First Dynasty.

Everted rim - A rim that is turned out from the body of a vase or pot. In Predynastic times, these rims were usually formed separately and attached to the body of the vessel.

Faience - A technique of decorating earthenware with opaque colored glazes.

Fancy ware - A grouping of pottery characterized by vessels in animal shapes and other "fanciful" decoration. Named by Petrie.

Fire dogs - Vertical supports or mudbrick andirons placed in the kiln to stabilize large vessels containing smaller pots.

Flint knapping - The technique of shaping flint by breaking off small pieces in order to form tools and implements.

Gerzean Period - (ca. 3500/3400-3200 B.C.) Named for the site, el Gerzeh, this was a time of increasing foreign influence. The introduction of a new red-on-buff painted pottery featuring realistic representations of processions of boats carrying shrines as well as geometric motifs; the use of fine ripple-flaked flint knives, animal effigy slate palettes, more widespread use of copper and precious metals such as gold and silver and the reduction of the extent of blackening around the tops of the standard red ware vessels reflect the influx of foreign influences.

29. Jar with Animal Face; Middle-Late Gerzean; (c) 1987 The Detroit Institute of Arts (90.1S12964); Gift of Frederick K. Stearns.

10. Dish; Amratian; Royal Ontario Museum, Toronto (900.2.103).

Hand-turning - A process of forming pottery by rotating the pot on a tournette or stand. Marks left on the rim of pots indicate this process.

Hanging Vase - A vase with applied handles on either side of the vase. The handles have lengthwise narrow or "string" holes. These vases were thought to have been suspended.

Hathor - The goddess of the Nile was depicted as having a cow head. She was also the goddess of fertility.

Heredotus - A Greek geographer who chronicled Egyptian times in about 450 B.C.

Hollow base point - A projectile point with a concave depression across the base.

Hor-Aha - King of the First Dynasty. He was possibly the son or grandson of Narmer.

Horus - The son of Re, Horus is frequently depicted as a hawk. The eye of Horus was lost during a fight with Set and was thought to be possessed with magical powers.

Hyksos - Western Asian people who conquered Northern Egypt in Middle Kingdom time.

Iconography - The traditional images or symbols associated with a subject.

Irj-Hor - One of the early kings of Egypt.

Khasekhemui - The last king of the Second Dynasty. With the end of his rule, the Archaic Period came to a close. It is thought that he may have ruled with Hierakonpolis as his capital for a time.

Lacustrine - Pertaining to or formed by a lake.

Late class (L-class) - Considered an unacceptable grouping of pottery by present archaeologists, this class groups various fabrics and surface treatments including: straw-tempered wares, marl wares, red-slipped and washed wares.

Leather-hard - The drying stage of pottery when the clay can be burnished with a smooth tool to a shiny surface.

Lower Egypt - The northern area of Egypt extending from the apex of the Nile Delta to the Mediterranean coast.

Macehead - A carved stone that was attached to a handle. The macehead symbolized power and was carried by chiefs, kings and then pharaohs. As time progressed the maceheads were decorated and commemorated significant events as is the case of the Scorpion macehead.

Malachite - Copper carbonate used in the eye paint of the Egyptians. It is green in color.

Manetho - A native Egyptian priest who wrote a history of Egypt for the Macedonian ruler, Ptolemy II, about 280 B.C. In his history, he devised a chronological scheme of dynasties or "ruling houses" to group the Pharaohs.

Marl - A fine calcareous clay that forms the soft shales in the desert wadis.

Naqada Period - Named for the Nubian site, Naqada, the period is separated into three recognizable changes in culture which parallel Amratian, Gerzean and Protodynastic periods.

Narmer - The first identified King of the united lands of Egypt. He may have been Menes whom the Greeks credited with this historic event. His name translates to "Catfish."

Neith - A beautiful goddess who was the protectress and patron deity of the city of Sais.

Neutron activation analysis - The activity of neutrons in an artifact are compared with the known activity in dated artifacts to estimate its age.

Nome - A province in Egypt.

Nubia - Located south of Aswan and running as far as the Second Cataract region in the Sudan, this narrow valley is the home region of the Pharaohs of the 25th Dynasty.

Nubian ware (N-class) - Distinctly different from later Egyptian pottery, Nubian pottery does have some similar characteristics to early Neolithic and Badarian pottery. Named by Petrie.

Nummulitic limestone - Widespread Upper Eocene Epoch (40-36 million years ago)limestone containing foraminifers (a very small spiral-shaped seashell). This rock is found in Europe, around the Mediterranean and in Northern Africa.

Osiris - Frequently seen in mummy form, Osiris is the King of the Underworld.

Palette - Purely functional in Predynastic times, palettes were used to grind eye pigment; or later in writing, to grind writing pigments. They took on a ceremonial purpose, such as in the Narmer Palette, and commemorated important events.

Petrie's Sequence dating - In trying to date and organize the multitudes of artifacts, Sir Flinders Petrie first identified distinctive styles and devised a system of relative dating, which dates the artifacts based on the evolution of the various forms. He termed this "Sequence Dating" and based the structure on the increase and decrease in frequency of styles of pottery and other objects found in the graves. A chronology and framework was then established for Upper Egyptian Predynastic cultures. While the system has been revised, it is still the basis of the present system.

Pharaoh - The Egyptian name of king derives from the term *Per-aa* or "Great House."

Polished Red Ware (Plum Red Ware or P-class) - Closely allied with black-topped red ware, the treatment of the surface is similar although there is no black rim. The

7. Double Jar; Amratian; Royal Ontario Museum, Toronto (900.2.11).

surface is polished with a stone or other smooth tool during the leather-hard stage to give the pot a burnished surface. The surface areas of the pot are then coated with red ocher before firing.

Porphyry - Igneous rock containing large and small crystals.

Predynastic - (4000-3100 B.C.) Direct ancestor of Dynastic culture.

Radio geochemical analysis - A group of tests which can be performed to date and analyze various substances in the artifact.

Re - Symbolized by the sun disk, Re was probably one of the most important deities of the Egyptian pantheon. The sun god had other forms he sometimes assumed, including the khepher or scarab beetle.

Red Land - The Egyptian's name for the desert, translated from the word *"deshru."*

Register - The Egyptians divided the palettes, wall paintings and other elements into a series of horizontal or vertical bands or divisions.

Rough ware (R-class) - Coarse pottery fired to light brown-to-orange color. These vessels are believed to have been utilitarian and are not normally found in grave sites. There is no surface treatment, but occasional incised lines decorate the vessels. Named by Petrie.

Scorpion - A Predynastic king.

Stela - A commemorative grave marker.

Tang - A projecting shank or prong.

Tawy - The ancient Egyptian term for the two lands of Upper and Lower Egypt.

Thebes - The capital of ancient Egypt and now the modern city of Luxor.

Theriomorphic - Having the shape of an animal.

Upper Egypt - The area of Southern Egypt extending from near Aswan to near present day Cairo.

Ushabti - Small models of servants which were placed in the tombs to magically carry out their duties for the dead. They were usually carved from wood and were prevalent in the Middle and New Kingdoms.

Wavy-handled (W-class) - Now considered a misnomer, this class consists of vessels with two wavy-shaped handles applied on opposite sides of the pot. Named by Petrie.

White cross-lined pottery (C-class) - This polished red ware is painted with light linear decorations in calciferous clay paint. Named by Petrie.

X-ray fluorescence - An analytical process used to identify the elements present in an artifact.

8. Bowl; Amratian; The Petrie Museum, University College London (UC 15353).

INDEX